THE REAL ESTATE INVESTOR'S POCKET CALCULATOR

THE REAL ESTATE INVESTOR'S POCKET CALCULATOR

SIMPLE WAYS TO COMPUTE CASHFLOW, VALUE, RETURN, AND OTHER KEY FINANCIAL MEASUREMENTS

Michael C. Thomsett

AMACOM

American Management Association

New York • Atlanta • Brussels • Chicago • Mexico City • San Francisco
Shanghai • Tokyo • Toronto • Washington, D.C.

Special discounts on bulk quantities of AMACOM books are available to corporations, professional associations, and other organizations. For details, contact Special Sales Department, AMACOM, a division of American Management Association, 1601 Broadway, New York, NY 10019.
Tel.: 212-903-8316. Fax: 212-903-8083.
Web site: www.amacombooks.org

This publication is designed to provide accurate and authoritative information in regard to the subject matter covered. It is sold with the understanding that the publisher is not engaged in rendering legal, accounting, or other professional service. If legal advice or other expert assistance is required, the services of a competent professional person should be sought.

Library of Congress Cataloging-in-Publication Data

Thomsett, Michael C.
    The real estate investor's pocket calculator : simple ways to compute cashflow, value, return, and other key financial measurements / Michael C. Thomsett.
        p.   cm.
    Includes index.
    ISBN 0-8144-7296-6
    ISBN 978-0-8144-7296-5
    1. Real estate business—Mathematics—Problems, exercises, etc.
2. Calculators—Problems, exercises, etc.   I. Title.

HF5695.5.R3T486   2006
332.63'24'0151—dc22

                                                                    2005018427

Printing number

10   9   8   7   6   5   4   3   2   1

CONTENTS

The Real Estate Investor's Pocket Calculator

THE BASIC
FINANCIAL PROBLEM

MORE THAN MOST INVESTMENTS, real estate requires the mastery of finance, valuations, and calculations. The very question of whether a particular investment is feasible relies on an understanding of how to calculate cash flow, income taxes, market forces, financing, and investment yield—the components of *value*.

The range of financial topics that are involved in finding, buying, and managing real estate investments is significant. This book breaks down the daunting range of tasks into a series of focused chapters, explains how the important measurements of value and feasibility are made, and explains how you then apply the information to smart decision making.

The study of real estate involves a broad range of topics, including the very basic concept of how real estate value is arrived at, how it changes, and what forces are at work in the market. That's the subject of Chapter 1. This leads to Chapter 2, where you will be able to compare appraisal methods used in setting and comparing valuation. Chapter 3 examines the calculations needed to study and compare mortgages, including an examination of how interest affects your profits. In Chapter 4, you will find a collection of important investment calculations and discover how they will help you in managing real estate. Chapter 5 discusses the lease option, a creative alternative to buying outright.

Most real estate investors need to rent out their properties to cover their debt service, so Chapter 6 is devoted to the financial aspects of renting. For those who are not interested in direct ownership or in being a landlord, Chapter 7 explains the many market alternatives, such as pooled investments. Chapter 8 provides useful guidelines for setting up a bookkeeping system for your real estate investments, and Chapter 9 provides details on how prorated values are used in real estate. In Chapter 10, proration is expanded to show how escrow calculations are completed. Chapter 11 takes a detailed look at the tax rules for real estate. Finally, in Chapter 12, you will find a good summary of how land and building measurements are done.

The book also has a series of useful appendixes. The first one, Appendix A, explains how mathematical conversion works and includes useful tables. Appendix B summarizes all of the formulas introduced throughout the book. Appendixes C and D provide amortization and remaining balance tables. Finally, you will find a detailed glossary of real estate terms.

Taken all together, this book provides you with a full range of financial calculation tools and demonstrates how they can be used to help you maintain control over your real estate investments. While many consider this topic to be complex, the material is organized in a way that makes it all quite clear. Through the use of examples, definitions, worksheets, and tables, the explanations are made as visual as possible, so that the information is far more than a series of explanations; it is intended to help you make decisions based on accurate facts. Too many individuals begin investment programs without truly understanding the risks involved and, of greater concern, without knowing what questions to ask before committing capital. In this book, you will not only see *how* specific calculations are done, but also find examples to demonstrate *why* those calculations are so essential.

CHAPTER 1

VALUATION OF PROPERTY

THE STARTING POINT

ALL INVESTMENTS ARE JUDGED on the basis of their current and future market value. In the case of real estate, the historical rise in the market value of properties has been consistent and has served as the base for many long-term financial plans. Many people, whether they are investing only in their own homes or expanding into a portfolio of rental properties, have discovered the potential for profits through real estate.

All forms of investing should be based on study and analysis. Real estate properties vary greatly in cost as well as in quality, location, and income potential. A smart place to begin the search for real estate investments is to identify some of the common myths about this market. These myths include the following:

1. *Real estate values always go up.* Markets always move in cycles. Therefore, every market—including the real estate market— will exhibit periods of strong growth and periods of stagnation and even decline in market values. While these cyclical changes may be temporary, they are part of the investing process.

2. *Profit over the long term is the most important criterion.* While profits are important to all investors, most people who put their money in real estate cover the majority of the purchase price through financing. Because investors have to generate enough rental income to cover their mortgage payments (along with

property taxes, insurance, utilities, and repairs), profits are only one of the measures by which the value of an investment is judged. Of far more immediate concern is the *cash flow* that you can gain from that investment. As long as rents are high enough to cover all of your expenses and payments, cash flow is positive. But if rents stop or aren't high enough to provide that coverage, your investment plan could be in trouble. This is where careful planning and analysis of risks is so important.

3. *Tax benefits are so good that it's always smart to carry a mortgage.* A common belief is that a mortgage—even one with a high interest rate—is beneficial as long as rental income is higher than the mortgage payments. The argument may be made that interest on the mortgage payment is deductible as an investment expense, so it does not make sense to pay down that mortgage or to get a lower balance initially. This is false. It is always better to reduce your payments and expenses; you will always end up with a stronger cash position with a smaller mortgage and lower payments.

4. *You can't lose with real estate.* It would be more accurate to say that the chances of losses on *any* investment are drastically reduced when you study the market beforehand. It is possible to lose money on any investment, but that invariably occurs because the real risks were not properly evaluated ahead of time. Real estate investors benefit from the historically strong market value growth in real estate, unique tax advantages for investors, cash flow potential from well-selected properties and well-screened tenants, and intelligent analysis in the selection of investment properties. In spite of advertising to the contrary, success in any form of investing is rarely easy or simple. It can be made so with research, which gives you an advantage over most investors.

WHERE AND WHEN TO BUY

The two factors determining real estate value are *location* and *timing*. When you begin to study the market, you start out with a large field. Just as a stock market investor starts with a potential investment field consisting of thousands of stocks, real estate investors also face a large number of possibilities and need to narrow down their choices.

Location and timing are concepts that are broadly understood by investors. In the stock market, you have market sectors, size of companies, capital strength, and competitive factors; these are the "locational" aspects of picking stocks. In real estate, location means the specific property and its immediate neighborhood, and also the city or town and larger region where the property is located.

With all investments, timing is everything. If you invest money when prices have peaked, your timing is poor; but the tendency among investors is to have the most enthusiasm and confidence at exactly those moments. If you invest money when prices are depressed, your timing *might* be good (only time will tell). But the tendency among investors is to be cautious and uncertain when prices have fallen. So the old advice to "buy low and sell high" applies to all markets, including the real estate market.

You face some artificial indicators when you look at real estate valuation. In a generally strong market, there may be a tendency to believe that *all* real estate is going to appreciate and that it is impossible to go wrong. Of course, you may see the same false euphoria in the stock market; but in real estate, regional trends may support this belief. Because real estate does not trade on an open exchange like stocks, it is difficult to spot short-term trends or to quantify them, and it is even more difficult to narrow down the location of a sensible real estate purchase.

These artificial indicators can mislead you if, in the search for valid data about the local market, you do not distinguish between broad and narrow forms of analysis. Mistakes in this area are of three types:

1. *Reviewing regional or national data on real estate trends.* The information about real estate that is easiest to find comes from sources like the National Association of Realtors (www.realtor.com) or the U.S. Census Bureau (www.census.gov). Both of these sources are extremely valuable for all real estate investors, but the statistical and demographic real estate trends reported on these sites are regional and national. Real estate investors

need to get down to the market supply and demand factors right in town. Average pricing trends for a section of the country or the entire nation are not of any use in timing a decision to buy investment real estate. All trends are local.

2. *Application of irrelevant data to the specific market.* If you are interested in buying rental property, you should also make sure that you study the applicable data. For example, if you want to purchase a fourplex and rent out its units, the decision should be made on the basis of prices, rental rates, and demand trends for similar properties. Local demand trends for single-family houses, raw land, or commercial property are not useful. While local trends for different types of real estate do tend to move in the same direction, there are no guarantees. Local economic forces, such as growth in jobs or an active tourist industry, may affect commercial property values, and increased prices of raw land may reflect a growing retirement demographic. At the same time, *rental* property may be lagging for a variety of reasons.

3. *Misreading one form of supply and demand when your concern should be for another.* The natural tendency of investors is to look to real estate because market values are rising. Most begin with the purchase of a single-family home as a rental. Some people move into this market when they decide to buy a larger home; instead of selling, they convert their present home to a rental with the idea that the tenants will "pay the mortgage" through rents. However, a strong demand for owner-occupied housing might not support a strong demand for rentals. It is possible that owner-occupied trends may be very strong, while rental demand is soft. These two markets are entirely separate. Factors influencing rental demand, even when single-family housing demand is strong, would include overbuilt apartment units. In that situation, housing prices may be rising at far above the national rate of inflation, while vacancy rates are high and market demand for rentals is soft. The supply and demand cycles for home ownership and for rentals are distinct and separate.

The question of where and when to buy is a strictly local one. It is not enough to study regional trends; you need to look at the trends in your city and, more specifically, in a particular neighborhood. Even in cities with only a few thousand residents, markets may differ vastly based on specific location. Before committing to real estate investments, it is essential to research the attributes of a neighborhood and how prices are trending, the types of rental demand and market prices for properties on a neighborhood-to-neighborhood comparative basis, and what factors influence those values (access to transportation, shopping, jobs, and schools, for example).

Analyzing real estate values requires comparative analysis, and many useful calculations certainly help. But as a starting point, you need to know the market firsthand. This is why a majority of first-time real estate investors tend to buy properties close to where they live. There are practical reasons for this, of course, but it simply makes sense to invest on familiar ground, literally speaking. You are most likely to understand the real estate trends within a few blocks of your own home and far less likely to understand the forces at work somewhere else, even in a city or town only a few miles away.

THE REAL ESTATE CYCLE

It may be fair to observe that there are two separate real estate cycles. The first is the theoretical or academic version that is studied in economics graduate classes; the second is the real cycle that is witnessed (or suffered) by real estate investors, builders, and developers.

Why are these different? The mathematical models of cyclical forces are useful to students whose exposure to economic forces is limited or nonexistent. Most students in economics graduate classes have never owned real estate or put money at risk in any other meaningful way, so, appropriately, their comprehension of real estate cycles will be based on theory rather than on practical experience. But *experience* provides investors with a far more pragmatic understanding of how money is made or lost. You see this in the stock market. Thousands of American investors jumped on the dot-com fad and bought shares of Internet stocks, many of which had never reported a profit. When the fad ended and many of those companies went out of business, investors lost money. For many people, this was the first time they had invested money. Having never had a loss before, it came as a cruel shock—but this is the reality.

In real estate, the same disparity is going to be found in first-time investors. While the market and its attributes are quite different from the stock market's dot-com fad, the same caution applies. The theoretical real estate cycle is not going to dictate how the real cycle operates, in terms of how long a cycle lasts or how far the cycle swings. Real cycles are characterized by short-term changes—misleading indicators, stagnation, and random movement. It is a mistake to attempt to time purchases through observation of current cycles. These cycles—varying degrees of supply and demand—are constantly shifting back and forth, and it is difficult to anticipate cyclical movements accurately. Both supply and demand contain a vast number of market components that can be understood best in a broader view, using historical information to follow trends and looking at moving averages. It is rarely possible to gain an absolutely clear view of current market conditions. It makes more sense to make investment decisions based on the fundamental strengths or weaknesses of the market (price trends in the immediate neighborhood, comparable sales prices of property, strength of rental demand, and so on). You should remember the observation, "Experience is the name everyone gives to their mistakes."[1]

To demonstrate how the difference between theory and reality play out, review the illustration of the real estate cycle shown in Figure 1.1.

The well-known economic identification points are shown in a falling and then a rising trend: recession, bottom, recovery, then expansion, top, and contraction. This model uses a base value that begins and ends in the same place. However, if prices are trending upward over a period of time, it is more likely that the base value will rise as well. In other words, while these cyclical phases will occur, the beginning and ending points will not be identical. This is illustrated in Figure 1.2.

Note that the overall value of real estate in this more realistic

---

[1] Oscar Wilde, *Lady Windermere's Fan*, 1892.

Figure 1.1.   The Supply and Demand Cycle.

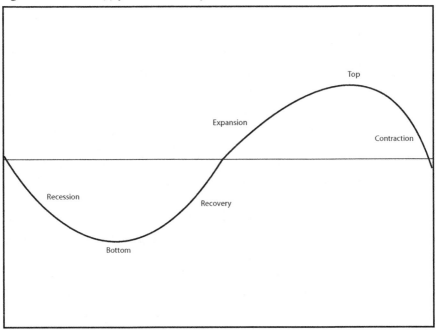

Figure 1.2.   The Supply and Demand Cycle with Moving Base Values.

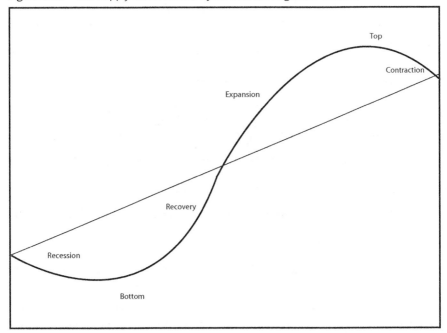

cyclical pattern rises over time, even while the forces of supply and demand interact and change. Stock market analysis may be realistically based on a set price level, and observers may experience times when prices are higher or lower than that level. Or price trends for stocks may also rise. In any market, the tendency for long-term price averages to evolve is a fair assumption, and the supply and demand cycle acts within that longer-term value trend.

Another important variation to note is the timing of a cycle. In the illustrations, the recessions and expansions are identical in length, indicating that these forces of change are somehow predictable. In practice, however, real estate cycles may be completed very rapidly (in a year or less as a form of mini-cyclical change), or they may evolve over many years. In addition, the recession and expansion phases are not necessarily equal in length. Recession may occur very gradually and expansion in a far shorter period, or vice versa. The aspect of cyclical analysis that is the most interesting, in fact, is the uncertainty. When you study cyclical patterns, you even out the timing and the false starts or stops along the way.

Cycles are best understood when they are analyzed broadly and with the use of averages. In practice, however, supply and demand changes do not act in "average" ways. The actual movement of the supply and demand cycle is more often far more chaotic and random.

JUDGING VALUES LOCALLY

The study of economic supply and demand cycles helps you to appreciate the interactions between buyers (demand) and sellers (supply). However, the analysis of real estate has to be based on local trends, not on regional or national cycles. When you hear statistics on housing starts, population ownership levels in real estate, or average prices of single-family homes, you need to put that information in perspective. National and regional trends are interesting, but they do not reveal what is happening in town.

Local values and trends are far more important to you as an individual investor. The starting point in any analysis should be identifying the market area where you expect to operate. The *market area* for real estate is not *all* real estate, nor is it a specific type of real estate, such as a single-family home. The applicable market area is a specific type of property located in a very specific locale with a price that is within a narrow range. An integral part of your market research is gaining an understanding of local rental demand levels and market rents.

On the individual property level, you start by looking at the land, the condition of the building, and the surrounding neighborhood. The age of the property and the condition of surrounding properties is revealing, because it provides an idea of whether current owners have performed ongoing maintenance, both for the property for sale and for the entire area. Neighborhoods tend to go through transitions, so condition may be a key indicator in identifying the best time to buy in an area. For example, one area may have many homes owned by older retired people whose children have grown and moved; as these older residents pass away, the homes are purchased by a new generation of first-time home buyers. (Many first-time buyers purchase older properties because they are more affordable, and later trade up to newer, more recently constructed homes; while this is a generalization, it is especially true when newer homes are significantly more expensive than older stock.) In this situation, older homes may be far out of date in terms of heating, electrical, and plumbing systems; roofs and paint; and the yard. So as new owners buy these homes, a positive transition of upgrades, renovations, and improvements begins to occur. This is a positive change because as older homes are brought up to date, they also tend to increase in value. Buying homes in neighborhoods that are in the early stages of positive transition is smart timing.

A negative transition occurs when owners begin moving away to other towns or neighborhoods, often because of undesirable changes. These include increasing crime, added noise resulting from new freeways nearby, or high-impact zoning changes close to the area. For example, when a state decides to run a new freeway through an existing town, it may cut an older neighborhood in half, so that one side becomes isolated from the other. This changes the character of both sides and may also lead to a decline in the market value of housing—a trend exacerbated by the noise resulting from a new freeway. When neighborhoods are going through a negative transition, you may find abandoned homes or empty lots because there is no financial incentive to build in the area, and it may be equally difficult to find suitable tenants. Crime may increase as well as people move out to escape ever-growing problems. Property values decline in such areas, so you may find "bargain" prices as well as good financing. However, because of the trends that are underway, it is not sensible to buy properties in these areas. It is likely that property values will continue to decline, possibly over many years.

The transitional test is a good starting point in comparing valuation. To help identify the many specific areas that collectively define the direction a transition is taking, check Table 1.1.

While the apparent transition for a single property may not tell the whole story, comparing the trends in several different neighborhoods and among a number of different properties will help in making distinctions. The selection of a property should be based on a combination of factors adding up to good value for the money: market value potential, good price and financing, safe neighborhood, and more. If you will be using the property as a rental, it also makes sense to check local market rental rates. The condition of the neighborhood determines (1) the market rate for rents, (2) the occupancy level you can reasonably expect to see, and (3) the kind of tenants who will apply.

MARKET CONDITIONS AFFECTING VALUE

Checking the property and the neighborhood is a smart test, but it is only the beginning. Once you find one or more properties that seem to be well priced, the next step is to evaluate the overall local market. What is the current state of supply and demand? Is the market currently a buyer's marker or a seller's market? What trends are going on now, and what should you expect in the near future?

If you ask a real estate agent these questions, you may not get a completely accurate answer. As a general observation, agents (whose compensation is commission-based) tend to tell buyers that this is the best time to buy, and to tell sellers that this the best time to sell. They are motivated to generate sales, and that requires that both sides come to the table. It would be rare for a real estate agent

Table 1.1.   Neighborhood Transitions.

Positive Transition	Negative Transition
Crime:	**Crime:**
Local statistics are promising	Local statistics are negative or unavailable
The area is clean and well maintained	There are empty lots, graffiti, and boarded-up homes
Police reports show a decline in crimes	Police report rising crime, notably in felony classifications
Employment:	**Employment:**
Job growth is strong	Jobs are being lost
The area encourages new companies to relocate there	Companies are closing and leaving the area
Unemployment is steady or falling	Unemployment is rising
Hazards:	**Hazards:**
Hazardous conditions are fixed quickly	Hazards are left or take a long time to remove
Zoning rules are enforced	A lot of mixed zoning is evident
Health care:	**Health care:**
The area is noted for excellent facilities	There is a shortage of adequate care facilities
Hospitals and clinics are conveniently located	Residents travel elsewhere for health care services
Citizens have voted for hospitals and Emergency Medical Services	Hospital and emergency systems are overloaded
Home maintenance levels:	**Home maintenance levels:**
Good care is taken by area homeowners	Homes and gardens are poorly maintained
Many homes are being upgraded and renovated	Properties are outdated and maintenance deferred
Few ''for sale'' or ''for rent'' signs are seen	Many homes are for sale or for rent
Noise:	**Noise:**
No traffic or other noise is evident	Local noise levels are high and noticeable
The area is generally quiet	Facilities (such as airports) are nearby
Parking:	**Parking:**
There is plenty of street parking available	Streets are too narrow; people park on lawns or gravel
Most homes have driveways	Few driveways are available

(continues)

Table 1.1.   (Continued.)

Positive Transition	Negative Transition
Traffic:	**Traffic:**
Traffic levels are low	Traffic is constant
People stick to the speed limit in the neighborhood	People speed without regard for safety
Traffic control is adequate given volume	Traffic piles up at stop signs and lights
Planning:	**Planning:**
Neighborhoods are well planned	Street patterns are haphazard
Yard areas are clean	Ordinances regarding unsightly gardens are not enforced
Types of property are consistent within areas	Many trailers, campers, and empty lots are evident
Buffer zones between zoning are maintained	Dissimilar zones seems to merge into one another
Residential lots are uniformly sized	Lot sizes vary considerably
Recreation:	**Recreation:**
Many desirable parks and playgrounds are seen	Few recreational areas are found
Existing recreational areas are nicely kept	Existing recreational areas are poorly kept
Statistics on sales:	**Statistics on sales:**
Home sales levels are consistent	Many homes are for sale
New homes and subdivisions are being built	No new construction is underway
Homes remain on the market only briefly	Homes sell and close rapidly
Public amenities:	**Public amenities:**
There are schools and shops nearly	Schools and shops are a distance away
Malls are well maintained	Malls are in disrepair, and many shops are empty
The downtown area is clean and robust	Downtown is virtually abandoned
Public transportation is efficient	Public transportation is slow and expensive

to tell a seller *not* to put a property on the market, or to discourage a potential buyer from looking at properties in the current market conditions.

To perform your own research on local market conditions, you need to dig a bit deeper and to study the trends on your own. Two good local sources for statistics, especially in the housing market, are local lenders and the area's Multiple Listing Service (MLS). Although MLS membership is usually restricted to people in the business, you should be able to find an agent who will allow you to review the sales statistics compiled by the local MLS office. Local MLS offices publish periodic summaries of homes for sale, with pictures and details, and summaries of recent statistical trends. This is where you find information that reveals the supply and demand conditions in today's local market.

CALCULATING SUPPLY AND DEMAND

The first step is to identify the *inventory* of homes on the market and then calculate the amount of supply that inventory represents. Inventory is simply the number of properties of each type that are for sale. For example, if you are interested in investing in single-family houses, you would not want to include commercial properties, apartment houses, or raw land; you would want to count only the inventory of houses currently for sale. Next, determine the average number of properties (in your category) that are sold each month. Divide the inventory (number of homes available) by the average number of closings that have occurred each month to find the number of months of housing inventory currently on the market.

Formula: Months of Property Inventory on the Market

$$\frac{I}{S} = M$$

where I = total inventory of properties currently available
       S = average sales per month
      M = months of inventory currently available

Like most forms of statistical analysis, the current number of months' inventory reveals only a part of the picture. Market conditions are clearly different in an area that has only two months' inventory versus another area with twelve months' inventory. However, you also want to track the *trend* in inventory. Is it growing or shrinking? Are there predictable seasonal considerations to keep in mind, and if so, what effect is predictable at each time of the year? Following the trend reveals the direction of the supply and demand cycle.

SPREAD

Two additional indicators found in MLS sales statistics are the *spread* between asked and sale prices and the amount of time between the original listing date and the closing date. By tracking the trends in these two important indicators, you can judge the strength or weakness of the market and assess both supply and demand conditions (as well as the direction and speed of the real estate cycle).

Spread is calculated by first determining the difference between asked and sale price, then dividing that difference by the original asked price. The result is expressed as a percentage. The sale price will most often be lower, so the spread is expressed as a negative percentage. For example, if a property was listed for $135,000 and sold for $129,500, the spread would be −4.2 percent (the difference of $5,500 divided by $129,500). In some markets (described as "hot" seller's markets), however, the sale price could be higher than the asked price. For example, a property listed at $135,000 may sell for $142,000. In this case, the spread would be expressed as a positive number, or +5.2 percent.

Formula: Spread

$$\frac{SP - AP}{AP} = S$$

where SP = sale price
       AP = asked price
       S = spread

TIME ON THE MARKET

The length of time a property is on the market is also a key indicator. The combination of spread and time on the market defines current supply and demand conditions and, of course, gains significance as an indicator when it is viewed as part of a trend. Remember, however, that this analysis is valid only when you restrict your study to the type of property you are analyzing. For example, if you are thinking of investing in single-family houses, you should exclude apartments and even duplexes or triplexes from your analysis of time on the market.

The analysis of time on the market is based on *completed* sales only. Thus, any listings that were withdrawn without being sold are not considered in this calculation. However, it may be useful and instructive to also track the number of withdrawn listings as a related indicator. To calculate time on the market, use the number of days. The alternatives (weeks or months) are more difficult to interpret. For example, 40 days versus 65 days is easier to comprehend than 6 weeks versus $9^1/4$ weeks, or $1^1/3$ months versus $2^1/6$ months.

Formula: Time on the Market

SD − LD = T

where SD = final sales date
     LD = original listing date
     T = time on the market (number of days)

VERIFYING VALUE WITH ASSESSMENT RATIO AND FINANCIAL INFORMATION

Most investors think of *value* in terms of profits. The difference between the purchase and sale price of a stock, bond, or property is, for many people, the single theme that defines whether a decision to invest had value.

While value defined as return on investment is crucial to the overall analysis of investing, other methods of quantifying value are equally important. The fundamental value of a property depends on timing within the real estate cycle, and timing may be defined by the inventory of properties, the spread between asked and sale prices, and the amount of time that property remains on the market. Beyond these measures, how can you test and compare value?

When an offer is made on a property, an appraisal is performed. This is normally a requirement of the lender, and it may not even occur until a serious buyer comes along. A smart seller may prepay for the appraisal and have it available to show to prospective buyers. This provides a means for demonstrating that the asked price is reasonable—especially if the appraisal value is higher.

ASSESSED VALUE

For rental properties, another method of verifying values is to check property tax bills and the local assessed value. Property tax bills show the property's assessed value, which is the value used to calculate the tax liability. This usually breaks down total value by land and improvements. Assessed value may lag well behind market value. In addition, assessed value is notoriously unreliable because of the time lag. If the local assessor's office is understaffed, inefficient, or even unqualified, assessments may reflect those problems as well.

With this in mind, checking assessed value for several different properties provides you with a comparison between assessed value and asked price. This is valuable information, since it may reveal inconsistencies or demonstrate an important difference between the realistic market value of properties and the basis used for property taxes. If nothing else, the analysis of assessed values is useful in determining whether those values are reliable from one part of town to another.

Formula: Assessment Ratio

$$\frac{P}{A} = R$$

where P = asked price
      A = assessed value
      R = assessment ratio

For example, suppose you check the assessed value for several properties on the market that you are thinking about purchasing. All are in the same city and are located in what you consider to be similar neighborhoods; the price ranges are similar as well. Comparing the assessed value to the asked price, you discover the relationships summarized in Table 1.2.

One problem with comparative analysis based on assessment values is that the age of those values may not be consistent. In many communities, for example, one-fourth of all properties are reassessed each year, on a revolving basis. This allows the city or county to keep its assessors' workload level each year. Thus, when comparing assessed value to asked price, you may also need to adjust the ratio to reflect the age of the assessment, based on historical increases.

In the previous example, 12 properties were reviewed and compared. Some disparities in assessment ratio were discovered; however, the age of the assessments varies between one and three years, so the comparison is not completely accurate. To correct this, a revised assessment ratio is required. The assessed value of each property should be increased by the average annual rise in assessed values in the community for each year since the latest assessment.

Formula: Assessment Ratio Adjusted

$$\frac{P(1 + i)^y}{A} = R$$

where P = asked price
      i = average annual increase in assessed value
      y = years since last assessment
      A = assessed value
      R = assessment ratio

Table 1.2.   Asked Prices and Assessed Value.

Property	Asked Prices	Assessed Value	Assessment Ratio
412 Elm St.	$107,500	$90,000	83.7%
95 Main St.	110,000	91,500	83.2
1440 – 23rd	113,200	94,500	83.5
29 Laurel	105,950	84,200	79.5
581 Indian Blvd.	112,000	93,000	83.0
44 Haynes	106,000	84,500	79.7
1132 B St.	105,500	91,000	86.3
40 Jackson Ave.	115,000	98,750	85.9
943 Green	109,900	90,350	82.2
8706 Valley Cove	112,000	96,000	85.7
3 Hayward Lane	102,490	86,000	83.9
564 Yates	110,650	95,000	85.9

By applying this formula to the properties in the previous example, you are able to approximate a more accurate comparison, as shown in Table 1.3.

With these adjustments, you arrive at estimates ranging between 82.2 percent and 87.5 percent, a considerable range. Recognizing that these are estimates only and not reliable as a means for judging the fairness of a property's price, you can nonetheless use this information to make comparisons. For example, if you divide the revised assessment by the average assessment ratio, you get an estimate of what the asked price should be (assuming that the calculated revised assessments are fair and comparable). If you take the extremes and compare, you arrive at:

44 Haynes	87,352 ÷ 85.2% = $102,526	
1132 B St.	92,365 ÷ 85.2% = $108,410	

From this, you could conclude that the asked price for 44 Haynes is high. It should be $102,526, but the actual asked price is $106,000. You may also conclude that 1132 B Street is a relative bargain at the asked price of $105,500.

Table 1.3.   Asked Prices and Assessed Value.

Property	Asked Prices	Assessed Value	Years	Revised Assessment*	Assessment Ratio
412 Elm St.	$107,500	$90,000	1	$ 91,350	85.0%
95 Main St.	110,000	91,500	1	92,873	84.4
1440 – 23rd	113,200	94,500	1	95,918	84.7
29 Laurel	105,950	84,200	3	87,042	82.2
581 Indian Blvd.	112,000	93,000	1	94,395	84.3
44 Haynes	106,000	84,500	3	87,352	82.4
1132 B St.	105,500	91,000	1	92,365	87.5
40 Jackson Ave.	115,000	98,750	1	100,231	87.2
943 Green	109,900	90,350	2	92,383	84.1
8706 Valley Cove	112,000	96,000	1	97,440	87.0
3 Hayward Lane	102,490	86,000	2	87,935	85.8
564 Yates	110,650	95,000	1	96,425	87.1
Average	$109,183			$ 92,976	85.2%

*Revised assessment based on average annual increases in assessed value of 1.5 percent per year. Thus, those properties assessed one year ago are estimated at 1.5 percent higher than reported assessed value; those with assessments two years ago are increased 2.25 percent (1.5 × 1.5), and those with assessments three years ago are increased 3.375 percent (1.5 × 1.5 × 1.5).

These estimates can be useful in comparing properties, especially if the assessment ratio is far off the average. However, you also have to remember that several other factors may distort the conclusion.

1. *Adjusted assessed value is only an estimate.* You cannot rely completely on what you discover from adjusting the assessed value. For example, in the previous comparison, one property was assessed last year, but the other had an assessment that was three years old. Using an average annual rate may distort actual assessed value.

2. *Specific attributes of the property may be a factor.* Even though two or more properties may be comparable in terms of both assessed *and* market value, attributes of those properties may affect both sides of the equation. These may include a den or office, an extra bathroom, the age and condition of the house itself, landscaping, the age of the roof, the heating and cooling system, or lot size, for example.

3. *Small changes between neighborhoods may affect assessed value.* What assessors and appraisers call "comparable" neighborhoods may be vastly different in many ways. Even small changes will have an effect, such as proximity to transportation, schools, and shopping; high noise levels due to highways or airports; crime and safety levels; traffic flow; the mix of neighbors (by age, owner-occupied versus rentals, or family size); and zoning (single-family residential versus mixed residential or higher-density zoning, for example).

4. *Seller motivation may also be a factor in how the asked price is set.* Finally, you have to also consider the variable of how motivated the seller is to close the deal. Some people are firm in their price and will not accept offers below that level. Others may be anxious to sell and may have priced their homes below the appraised value to generate a fast sale.

Another source of information concerning value of a property is the seller's tax return. This applies if the property in question has been used as a rental property; if the seller has used the house as a primary residence, there will not be any value in reviewing the tax return.

For rental properties, rents and expenses are reported on federal Schedule E. If you are thinking of purchasing a property that has been used as a rental, ask to see the seller's Schedule E for the last two or three years. This enables you to judge the amounts of rent collected (net of vacancies, if applicable) and the level of recurring expenses involved: utilities, maintenance and repairs, property taxes, and landscaping.

Making a comparison between properties will be impossible if some properties were not used as rentals. In these situations, you need to estimate a comparable rental income and expense level based on mortgage payment levels and interest rates, property tax expenses, utilities, and market rents you expect to receive. Another potential problem is a seller's refusal to show you any part of a tax return. However, this is also a matter of the seller's motivation. If the property has been a profitable rental, then the Schedule E record will help complete the sale. If the seller is reluctant to disclose this information, it may be a sign that the property is not as attractive as an investment because of high maintenance or utilities expenses, vacancies, or other factors. If sellers are not willing to show you their property financial statements, that is itself a warning sign. After all, the request is reasonable. If you were thinking of buying a retail business from someone, you would expect to see the financial statements. The Schedule E is a financial statement for a rental property.

EXPENSE RATIO

In addition to checking average annual rents, you will also be interested in checking the expense ratio between properties. Also called the operating ratio, this is a comparison between operating expenses and rental income. *Operating expenses* are the ongoing expenses of the property without including interest on the mortgage. Because interest varies based on rate, down payment, length of the mortgage term, and the beginning mortgage balance, it would not be accurate to use the owner's average interest when comparing one property with another. So the operating ratio includes expenses other than interest on the debt; owner-paid utilities, property taxes, insurance, repairs and maintenance, and landscaping are typical. The ratio is expressed as a percentage, and it is most valuable when two or more properties are being compared.

Formula: Expense Ratio

$$\frac{E}{I} = R$$

where E = operating expenses
I = gross income from rents
R = expense ratio

RETURN ON INVESTMENT AND EQUITY CALCULATIONS

A final version of *value* that is of special interest to real estate investors is the more traditional calculation of rate of return or return on investment. The various methods of calculating return may be used to judge results between properties, to set minimum standards, or to compare returns between real estate and other types of investments (savings accounts, mutual funds, or stocks, for example).

Two specific types of investment return calculations are important to investors: return on investment and return on equity. Return on investment is the return based on the amount of cash invested; it provides you with comparative information on how well you have "put your money to work" in the selection of products (real estate, savings, stocks, and so on). Return on equity is different. This is the return based on the value of an investment. In the case of real estate, equity is likely to change over time, as a result of improved market value and periodic mortgage payments to principal. This is an important measurement for all investments, because it provides you with a quantified comparative look at a particular investment's success. To understand return on equity, consider what happens if a property's market value is growing at a faster rate than the relatively slow pace of payments to principal on a loan. For example, suppose that a property's market value is growing at 3 percent per year. Assuming a 20 percent down payment on a $150,000 purchase, the changes over 30 years will be quite different for investment and for equity. And in this comparison, *return* would be based on a sale price for the property or on an estimate of what that sale price would be.

RETURN ON INVESTMENT

To calculate return on investment, first estimate the total amount of cash that would be received upon sale of the property. This may be a complex number to estimate. You need to first assume the sale price, then deduct closing costs and the overall federal and state tax liabilities to arrive at the *net* cash you would receive upon sale. Of course, if you are calculating return on investment after the sale, you have the actual numbers available.

Once you determine the amount of cash received upon sale, deduct the cash-based investment in the property. This consists of your down payment plus the equity accumulated through payments on your mortgage loan. For example, on a $120,000 loan at 7 percent amortized over 30 years, your total principal payments after 10 years would be about $17,000. Added to a down payment of $30,000, your investment in the property would be $47,000.

The next step is to deduct the cash investment from the net cash received. This is the overall return on your investment. However, to make the calculation accurate, you also need to annualize the return, or reflect the return on average per year. This is necessary because it makes a difference when two properties produce the same return on investment, but one was held for five years and the other for ten.

Formula: Return on Investment

$$\frac{P - O}{O} = R$$

where P = proceeds upon sale
       O = original investment
       R = return on investment

Annualizing the return for any calculation involves restating the return for the entire holding period on an *average* annual basis—as if the investment were held for exactly one year. For investments held only a few months, use the number of months or days that the investment was owned. For longer periods, use years. In the following formula, the return (*R*) may represent a return on investment over a holding period (*H*) of 10 years. Thus, the average annual return (*A*) would involve dividing the return by 10.

Formula: Annualized Return (Using Years)

$$\frac{R}{H} = A$$

where R = return over entire holding period
        H = holding period (number of years)
        A = annualized return

When annualized return involves a calculation using months, you would divide the overall return by the number of months held and multiply the result by 12 (months).

Formula: Annualized Return (Using Months)

$(R \div H) \times 12 = A$

where R = return over entire holding period
        H = holding period (number of months)
        A = annualized return

This formula works in situations where investments are held for periods shorter or longer than one year. For example, consider the following comparison: In one case, you held an investment for 8 months and received an overall return on investment of 7 percent. In another case, you held the property for 14 months and also received a 7 percent return:

1. $(7 \div 8) \times 12 = 10.5$ percent

2. $(7 \div 14) \times 12 = 6.0$ percent

The outcome in the two cases is far different when you annualize the returns. The shorter holding period yields 4.5 percent more than the longer period, because of the annualization of the return.

RETURN ON EQUITY

Return on equity is far different from return on investment. The *investment* is defined as the amount of cash placed into the property, in the form of the original down payment plus periodic payments on the principal balance of the note. The investment basis has to be increased by the amount of any capital improvements, such as an addition, a new roof, or other major expenditures. For example, if you purchase a property for $150,000 and later add capital improvements that cost $25,000, your investment basis rises to $175,000. In comparison to *basis* in property, *equity* is the difference between the total value of the property and the amount owed on a mortgage loan.

Formula: Equity

$$V - B = E$$

where V = current market value
B = balance, mortgage debt
E = equity

Return on equity will also be calculated with different numbers. If you check back to the formula for return on investment, you will use a similar procedure, but instead of calculating your investment basis, you use current equity. For example, let's assume that you bought a property for $150,000 and put $30,000 down. After 10 years, you have accumulated another $17,000 worth of payments, so your total *investment* would be $47,000. At that point, you would still owe about $103,000 on the original $120,000 loan. If you could sell the property today for $250,000, your *equity*—the difference between the current market value and the remaining debt—would be $147,000 ($250,000 less $103,000). This does not take into account the cost of selling. If you want to calculate the *net* return on equity, you would first deduct the cost of selling from the current market value. This number is called *proceeds upon sale*.

Formula: Return on Equity

$$\frac{P - E}{E} = R$$

where P = proceeds upon sale
E = equity (net market value minus debt)
R = return on equity

▨ TRACKING RETURNS OVER TIME

Return on investment and return on equity reveal valuable but different types of information. However, you are not limited to studying value only at the point of sale or when you are thinking about selling. You can also track returns over time.

MOVING AVERAGE

Given the chaotic changes in the supply and demand cycle, viewing values or potential returns from one period to another without averaging out those returns is quite difficult. It is useful to investors tracking real estate values over time to use *moving averages*. This applies to following the market value of real estate, cash flow, and estimated return on equity.

With a moving average, you begin by selecting a *field* of values. For example, month-end or quarter-end average values of property in one city would provide you with an averaged view of movement in the real estate cycle. Then you add together the values in the field and divide the total by the number of fields. For example, if you track real estate values at the end of each quarter over three years (12 quarters), you add the values together and then divide by 12. In a typical moving-average analysis, the field is shifted with each new period, so that you always count the same number of fields. In the preceding example, you would always count the latest value, add it to the previous 11 values, and use the average to make the latest entry on a chart.

Formula: Moving Average

$$\frac{V_1 + V_2 + \cdots V_f}{N} = A$$

where V   = values in the selected field
      1, 2, . . . f = first, second, remaining, and final values
      N   = number of values in the field
      A   = moving average

WEIGHTED MOVING AVERAGE

In some circumstances, it is necessary to use a *weighted moving average*. This is applicable when the outcome will be more accurate than the outcome if you use a simple moving average. The theory behind weighting is that the latest information is more important than earlier, outdated information and should be given greater weight. There are many different ways to weight a moving average. For example, you may count each value except the most recent only once, but count the most recent value twice. That gives the most recent entry in the field twice the weight of the preceding values. If there are 12 values in the field and you double-weight the latest entry, you divide the total by 13 to arrive at a weighted moving average. Another method is to add ever-higher weight levels for each value, but this becomes far more complex when a lot of values are involved. For example, with 12 values, you would weight the latest entry by a factor of 12 and, as you move farther back, use weights equal to 11, 10, 9, and so on. The total would then be divided by 78, the sum of the digits of the weighted values (1 + 2 + 3 + 4 + 5 + 6 + 7 and so on). The formula used as an example weights the latest entry twice.

Formula: Weighted Moving Average

$$\frac{V_1 + V_2 + \cdots (V_f \times 2)}{N + 1} = A$$

where V = values in the selected field
1, 2, ... f = first, second, remaining, and final values
N = number of values in the field
A = weighted moving average

In this formula, the final value (the latest entry) is multiplied by 2 in order to give it greater weight. The entire field is then multiplied by the number of fields plus 1 (to account for the weighting). If the final value were weighted by a factor of 3, you would need to add 2 to the divisor because the number of values would be greater. For example, in a field of 12 values, weighting the latest entry by three times would bring the total up to 14; thus, using $N + 2$ (12 + 2) as the divisor would make the weighted average accurate.

EXPONENTIAL MOVING AVERAGE

Another method that provides a weighted value is called an *exponential moving average*. This is a fairly complex calculation, but it can be programmed using an Excel spreadsheet. The five steps in the formula are summarized here, using the example of six fields in the moving average, with values of 34, 22, 44, 62, 16, and 11; and with the latest value to be added in of 17:

1. Compute the *exponent* by dividing 2 by the number of fields in the moving average.

$$2 \div 6 = 0.333$$

2. Compute the average for the six previous entries.

$$\frac{(34 + 22 + 44 + 62 + 16 + 11)}{6} = 31.5$$

3. Subtract the latest value from the moving average to find the new value.

$$31.5 - 17 = 14.5$$

4. Multiply the new value by the exponent (from step 1).

$$14.5 \times 0.333 = 4.833$$

5. Add the result of step 4 to the previous moving average.

$$4.833 + 31.5 = 36.333$$

On an Excel spreadsheet, the same calculations would be summarized with formulas, as:

Excel Address	Value	Calculation to Use	Explanation
A1	6		Number of fields
A3	0.333	= SUM(2/A1)	Calculation of exponent
A6	34		Value 1
B6	22		Value 2
C6	44		Value 3
D6	62		Value 4
E6	16		Value 5
F6	11		Value 6
A8	31.5	= SUM(A6:F6)/6	Simple moving average

A10	17		Latest entry
A11	14.5	= SUM(A8-A10)	Prior moving average less latest entry
A13	4.833	= SUM(A11*A3)	Multiply by the exponent
A15	36.333	= SUM(B13 + B8)	Add to prior moving average to find new moving average

Formula: Exponential Moving Average

$$\left(\frac{V_1 + V_2 + \cdots V_f}{N} - L \right) \times \frac{2}{N} + \frac{V_1 + V_2 + \cdots V_f}{N} = NA$$

where V   = values in the selected field
1, 2, . . . f = first, second, remaining and final values
N   = number of values in the field
L   = latest entry
NA   = new moving average

Applying the formula to the previous example,

$$\frac{34 + 22 + 44 + 62 + 16 + 11}{6} - 17 \times (2 \div 6) +$$

$$\frac{34 + 22 + 44 + 62 + 16 + 11}{6} = 36.333$$

The exponential moving average may be excessively complex for most applications; however, it is instructive to know how to perform the calculation. Using the Excel spreadsheet formula, the exponential moving average is reduced to a calculation involving only a single new entry for each period. This reduces the complexity. For exceptionally long periods of study, the exponential moving average formula makes the moving average easier to manage. As with all types of formulas, even simple or weighted moving averages, the use of formulas on spreadsheets makes calculation easy and fast.

For most investors, valuation is a smart starting point. However, valuation itself is also a matter of detailed comparison among properties. Appraisers use a variety of methods to establish the market value of properties. These techniques are explained in Chapter 2.

HOW THE NUMBERS ARE MANIPULATED IN APPRAISALS

AN APPRAISER MAY BE an independent who works for a variety of attorneys, bankers, and lenders; an employee of a lending institution or real estate brokerage firm; or an employee working in a city or county assessor's office. All of the functions surrounding the appraisal of property (including not only residential property, but also commercial property, industrial property, and land) require training in the valuation of real estate.

Many organizations serve this large industry, some specifically for residential appraisers or assessors and others for more specialized professionals. You may need to locate an appraiser on your own if, for example, you want to have an independent appraisal in hand for a property you want to put on the market. You may also want to request that a lender use an appraiser referred by a specific membership organization.

Valuable resource:

To find the right appraiser for a real estate property for financing or valuation of residential or nonresidential properties, check the following Web sites:

Appraisal Foundation, http://www.appraisalfoundation.org, a membership organization that sets industry standards

Appraisal Institute, www.appraisalinstitute.org, a professional association for appraisers

National Association of Independent Fee Appraisers, http://www.naifa.com, an organization that awards the IFA designation and offers education courses for professional appraisers

National Association of Real Estate Appraisers, http://www.iami.org/narea.htm, an organization that provides subscribers with news on regulatory trends

Individuals may hire appraisers for numerous reasons other than financing the purchase or sale of property. For example, appraisals may be required as part of settling a deceased person's estate or requested by one or both sides in a divorce proceeding.

Like many professional reports, appraisals of property can be subjective within a range of possible valuation levels. There is no one set price that is absolute for property; in fact, by definition, the "price" of real estate is the amount a seller is willing to accept and a buyer is willing to pay. Many concessions and agreements can affect that price, including financing terms, inspections and repairs, closing dates, and contingencies placed on an offer. A property is likely to be valued within a range of possible prices, and an appraiser will be able to establish an opinion of the property's value based partially on the purpose of the appraisal. But it is an opinion. The professional appraiser needs to adhere to standards in arriving at that opinion, and the appraisal report has to be based on sound principles. So when appraisers compare a property to recently sold properties, those "comps" have to be similar in size, features, age, and neighborhood; and to the extent that there are variances, the appraiser documents the differences and adds or subtracts an estimated value to adjust the value of the subject property.

Why do appraisal levels vary? If a lender hires an appraiser to look at a property, the purpose of the appraisal is to ensure that the value of that property is in line with the price the buyer and seller have agreed upon. If the lender is conservative, the appraisal will probably reflect that conservatism, at least to some degree. Appraisal is neither exact nor precise enough for everyone to agree with an opinion concerning value, but the need to document and justify the final opinion makes appraisals convincing documents.

Many institutions and individuals depend on these reports and their reliability, including lenders, buyers, sellers, attorneys, and (in the case of assessments for property taxes) the city or county budget office.

The methods used by appraisers to set the value of property vary depending on the type of property and whether it is to be used for production of income or as a residence. When lenders review loan applications, owner-occupied housing is considered relatively safe, especially if the homeowner makes a sizable down payment. Thus, the appraisal may reflect the relative safety for the lender. However, investment property presents greater risks, which is why lenders require higher down payments and may also look for a more conservative appraisal.

THE COST APPROACH

Appraisers have flexibility in how they arrive at a valuation, but their conclusions have to be justified. So the appraisal report carefully documents how the appraiser arrived at the final opinion of a property's value. This involves comparing the property to recent sales or, in the case of income property, to the income levels generated by similar properties of the same size and type. There are three methods used by appraisers: the cost approach, the market or sales comparison approach, and the income approach.

For residential properties, appraisers use either the cost approach or the market or sales comparison approach; the two may also be combined in a single analysis, with greater weight being given to one method or the other, depending on the appraiser's opinion as to which outcome is more accurate.

The *cost approach* is a process of identifying value based on the question, "What would it cost today to build a house exactly like the subject property?" The appraiser estimates the cost of construction, deducts depreciation to reflect the wear and tear on the property, and then adds the value of the land.

Formula: Cost Approach

$$C - D + L = V$$

where C = cost of improvements
       D = depreciation
       L = land value
       V = value of the property

You need to understand how appraisers arrive at the components of the cost approach. The cost of improvements, depreciation, and land value are based on measurements of current costs and values as well as on the condition of the improvements.

The actual cost of improvements will vary by area. Construction costs are going to be far higher in some metropolitan areas than in others, and appraisers base their cost estimates on *local* costs rather than national averages. So as a starting point, appraisers measure the full area of a property to find the total square feet. In cases where there is a second floor, the appraiser needs to add additional square feet to estimate the total living space of the property. Also included will be attics, basements, garages, outbuildings, and porches.

The linear measurement of square feet does not take into account any special features of a property, such as exceptionally high ceilings. So appraisers may need to consider the internal amenities of a property, including use of space (or waste of space), design features, and other special features (fireplaces, stairs, and so on). As a starting point, the appraiser multiplies the total square feet by the cost of construction to arrive at an initial estimate of value. The cost for the house may be different from the cost for a garage or barn, so a different multiplier may be used. In addition, value has to be estimated for outside features such as landscaped garden areas, swimming pools, fenced pasture or agricultural land, and views. All of these features would lead the appraiser to adjust the cost of improvements based on both the cost and the estimated value of such improvements and features.

Depreciation for appraisal purposes is not the same as the depreciation formulas used as part of reporting income or loss on a tax return. The appraiser estimates depreciation based on the *effective age* and *economic life* of the property. Effective age is the current age of improvements based on their condition (not on their actual construction age). So a very well-maintained property will have a younger effective age than one that has been allowed to fall into disrepair. The economic life is an estimate that the appraiser uses to determine the total number of years over which improvements have value. For example, if a house is estimated to have an economic life of 50 years, that serves as the base from which the appraiser will calculate depreciation. The longer the economic life, the less depreciation will be deducted per year. So a property that was constructed with exceptional craftsmanship and has been well maintained will probably be depreciated at a slower rate than one with shoddy construction.

Formula: Depreciation (Appraisal)

$$\frac{100}{E} = D$$

where E = economic life
D = annual rate of depreciation

The appraiser needs to estimate the reasonable economic life based on experience and comparison among many properties. Calculating depreciation is essential to estimating the current net value of improvements. For example, if the appraiser believes that a particular property has an economic life of 40 years, the formula will calculate depreciation per year as:

$$\frac{100}{40} = 2.5\%$$

The cost to build new improvements would need to be reduced by 2.5 percent for each year of the effective age of the property to arrive at the current value. For example, if you assume that a property with an economic life of 40 years has an effective age of eight years, the net current value requires that the appraiser deduct eight years' worth of depreciation.

Formula: Net Current Value of Property

$$C - (C \times R \times E) = N$$

where C = cost
R = rate of depreciation
E = effective age
N = net current value

For example, let's assume that the appraiser sets a new cost of improvements at $80,000. The annual rate of depreciation is 2.5 percent (decimal equivalent 0.025) per year, and the effective age is eight years. (Both rate of depreciation and effective age are *estimates* made by the appraiser.) The calculation of net current value is:

$$\$80,000 - (\$80,000 \times 0.025 \times 8) = \$64,000$$

In this example, the appraiser estimated that the cost of new construction is $80,000, that depreciation had to be calculated at 2.5 percent per year, and that the effective age of the property was eight years. Thus, $16,000 is deducted for depreciation. Based on its condition and age, the current net value of this property is $64,000.

This method—like all appraisal methods—requires estimates. However, the appraiser uses a consistent methodology in estimating the condition, age, and cost value of properties. Under the cost method, the appraiser also has to estimate the value of the land. The preceding calculations referred only to improvements. To calculate the value of the land itself, the appraiser considers the topography, size, and shape of the property, then researches the value of similar land in the area.

If the appraiser can find identical lots that were recently sold, it is fairly easy to calculate the land value. Of course, this assumes that the lot is the same size, used in the same manner, and located in the same neighborhood or one just like it. In practice, it may be necessary to review three or more comparable sites and make adjustments up or down to estimate a fair market value. Estimates will be made for the typical reasons: topography, size, and shape. However, additional adjustments may also be made for differences in neighborhood, views, and amenities (such as the existence or lack of trees on the site, for example); noise levels resulting from nearby land uses (freeways or airports, for example); and proximity to schools and transportation. (A lot located across the street from a school might seem very convenient to a family with children; however, daytime noise levels may offset that value in an appraiser's opinion.)

The final step in the cost method is to add together the carefully documented value of improvements and land to arrive at a total estimated current market value. Appraisers may depend wholly on the cost approach or combine it with the market or sales comparison approach. The appraiser may also decide to give greater weight to one method or the other in arriving at a final market value estimate, based on opinion and experience.

THE MARKET OR SALES COMPARISON APPROACH

The *market or sales comparison approach* is widely used for appraisal of residential properties. It often is combined with the cost approach, with the final market value being based on both methods. This is a valid form of confirmation. If the cost and market or sales comparison approaches ended up with vastly different indicated values, it would indicate that the calculations were incorrect.

In employing both methods, appraisers may average the two, select one value over the other, or set a value that gives greater weight to either the cost approach or the market or sales comparison approach. It is a matter of judgment.

Under this method, the appraiser attempts to locate *comparable* properties that have sold recently in the same area or in neighborhoods with characteristics similar to those of the subject property. This is not always easy. A house that is atypical for a neighborhood is difficult to appraise; nonconforming features (oversized improvements, exceptionally large lots, more square feet than typical homes) tend *not* to be given their full potential value because those features and amenities are not standard for the area. So a 5,000-square-foot home on a double lot located in a neighborhood with 2,000-square-foot homes on single lots will not be appraised at a rate proportionately greater than the other homes in that neighborhood.

The appraiser will locate at least three properties considered to be comparable to the subject property. They should all have been sold within the past year, and more recent sales are preferable to older sales. A "comparable" series of features includes lot size, square feet of the property, number of rooms, age and condition, topography, and special features (extra bathrooms, remodeled kitchens, swimming pools, landscaping, fireplaces, outbuildings, den or office, or solar heating, for example). Some features add value at a rate well below their actual cost. For example, fencing and landscaping often do little to add value to property. Swimming pools are not always considered desirable, and some added features are valued based on local climate (e.g., fireplaces or solar heating).

The appraiser lists all of the features of the subject property and comparable properties, then adjusts the value of the subject property up or down based on differences. Any variation in features between the properties may result in an adjustment. For example, if condition of the subject property is superior to that of the comps, some value will be added to reflect less depreciation (in comparison to the recent sales levels of the comparable properties). The same goes for internal size of properties, features, and lot size. Adjustments are generally made to the sales prices of comparable properties as a means of determining average sales prices. For example, if the appraiser finds three comps and adjusts for a number of features, the following outcome may result:

Description	Comp 1	Comp 2	Comp 3
Sales price	$155,000	$162,000	$166,500
Location		−1,000	−3,000
Square feet	−2,000	−3,000	
Condition		−4,500	
Additional bath	+1,200		
Additional bedroom			−5,000
Outbuilding, storage	+3,200		
Comparable adjusted values	$157,400	$153,500	$158,500

The adjustments would reflect features on which the comps were superior to the subject property (resulting in additions to the sales price) or inferior (resulting in subtractions).

Formula: Market or Sales Comparison Approach

$$\left(\frac{C_1 + C_2 + \cdots + C_n}{N} \right) \pm A = V$$

where C   = comparable property values
       1, 2, ... n = comparable properties
       N   = number of comparable values
       A   = plus or minus adjustments
       V   = market value

In this example, the average comes out to:

($157,400 + $153,500 + $158,500) ÷ 3 = $156,467

The estimated value of the subject property may equal the average of $156,467, it may be rounded up or down, or the appraiser may set a value based not on the strict mathematical average but on the opinion that one of the comparable properties is more representative of overall market value than the others. For example, if comp 2 was most like the subject property, the appraiser could make a judgment that it should have greater influence than the other two properties. The subject property's value could be set at a level lower than the average. The appraiser might also decide to give greater weight to comp 3 because it required the least number of adjustments. There are many methods of justifying a final decision in the market or sales comparison approach.

THE INCOME APPROACH

The most complex of the three methods that appraisers use to set value for properties is the *income approach*. This is used to estimate market value for income-producing properties. It is more commonly used for multiunit residential properties and for commercial rental properties. The income approach can be used for single-family properties; however, an appraiser may prefer to use a combination of the cost and sales or market comparison approaches even when a property is used as a rental. If it is situated in a neighborhood of similar houses that are used as primary residences for the most part, it may not be accurate to estimate value based on income. However, if the property is located in an area dominated by single-family homes used as rentals (and with recent sales of properties generating rental income), the income approach may be appropriate.

The premise of the income approach is that recent sales of similar income-producing properties indicate value based on the gross income as the primary determinant. So the first step is to estimate the *economic rent* for the property. This is based on market rents for similar properties in the area. Depending on how the appraiser approaches the question of rent levels and on the available data, the market rent can be calculated based on total square feet, number of rooms, or number of units. Because an appraiser may be dealing with a variety of different types of properties (single-family homes, duplexes and triplexes, and apartments, for example), a consistent use of one method may be preferable.

Formula: Economic Rent per Square Foot

$$\frac{R}{S} = E$$

where R = rent per period
        S = square feet
        E = economic rent per square foot

Formula: Economic Rent per Room

$$\frac{R}{N} = E$$

where R = rent per period
        N = number of rooms
        E = economic rent per room

Formula: Economic Rent per Unit

$$\frac{R}{U} = E$$

where R = rent per period
        U = number of units
        E = economic rent per unit

Using the per-unit method as an example, the appraiser may use monthly or annual rent to calculate the next step, the *gross rent multiplier (GRM)*. This is a factor used for similar properties to identify the market value of the subject property. Using monthly rents as an example, the appraiser may study sales for several different properties in the same area over the past few months. In many areas, GRM averages are well understood by appraisers and real estate professionals; however, the appraisal methodology is an important step, if only to ensure that the proper range of comps is employed in the appraisal analysis. GRM is calculated by dividing the comparable property's sales price by the rent.

Formula: Gross Rent Multiplier

$$\frac{S}{R} = G$$

where S = sales price
       R = rent per period
       G = gross rent multiplier

An appraiser may discover the following, using monthly rent numbers:

Property	Sales Price	Monthly Rent	GRM
1	$150,000	$1,000	150.00
2	$144,500	$ 850	170.00
3	$153,950	$ 925	166.43
4	$149,900	$ 900	166.56
5	$148,000	$ 900	166.44
6	$152,000	$1,020	149.02
Average			161.41

This analysis shows that—as a general observation—higher-priced rentals may produce lower GRMs. For example, two properties that sold for at least $150,000 had GRM levels at 150 or below. The lower-priced sales tended to report higher GRMs. This reflects market tendencies among rental properties, especially in residential markets. Because people want to pay lower rents, they may also be willing to accept less in the way of room size, amenities, and condition.

The factor the appraiser settles upon would then be used to estimate the value of a property using the income approach. For example, if 161.41 were to be used and monthly rents per unit were $975, the property would be valued at

161.41 × $975 = $157,375

The GRM may also be calculated using annual rents. Repeating the previous example, but with *annual* rent levels, the analysis reveals

Property	Sales Price	Annual Rent	GRM
1	$150,000	$12,000	12.50
2	$144,500	$10,200	14.17

3	$153,950	$11,100	13.87
4	$149,900	$10,800	13.88
5	$148,000	$10,800	13.70
6	$152,000	$12,240	12.42
Average			*13.42*

The outcome using annual rent levels would be approximately the same as in the previous example:

13.42 × $11,700 = $157,014

In either case, the method has to be used consistently to arrive at a dependable GRM. For larger income-producing properties, a more complex income approach may be used, involving a comparison between rents and estimated returns from other investments, operating expenses, and depreciation. That includes calculating the internal rate of return and employing computerized calculation software. While appraisers may need to explore this formula in more detail, it is beyond the scope of this book.

Appraisers dealing with income property employ another standard, used to compare their estimated appraised values against local standards as well as other properties. The *capitalization rate* (popularly called the "cap rate") is derived by dividing annual net income by the purchase price (or by the assumed market value) of property.

Formula: Capitalization Rate

$$\frac{I}{P} = C$$

where I = annual net income
     P = purchase price
     C = capitalization rate

For example, you can take the calculation of GRM a step further. In the previous example, you saw that the annual GRM for an appraised property was 13.42, so that market value was:

13.42 × $11,700 = $157,014

What happens when you take the next step? Assuming that the property was purchased for $157,014, the cap rate would be based on calculated *net* income (not gross rents), and that outcome could be compared to the return on similar properties. For the would-be investor, this calculation answers the question, Is this property going to be a profitable investment? Based on comparisons to similar properties, the cap rate can be revealing. For example, if the property is to be purchased at $157,014 and net annual income has averaged $9,500 per year, the cap rate will be:

$$\frac{\$9{,}500}{\$157{,}014} = 6.1\%$$

How does this compare to typical cap rates in the area? If the appraiser determines that the average cap rate is 5.5 to 6.0 percent, this is a positive outcome; however, if cap rates have averages of 7 to 8 percent, then this property would underperform based on that standard.

VALUATION IN RENTAL PROPERTIES

Within the calculations of the income approach to appraisal, many subcalculations take place. While the nonincome approaches tend to be based on current market prices for properties, the income approach is far more complex.

Appraisers will also calculate the likely *profit margin* on income property, the result of dividing cash flow from comparable properties and the subject property by *effective gross income*. This is gross income adjusted for likely vacancies or concessions (e.g., free rent for one month in exchange for signing a one-year lease). The profit margin, because it is based on cash flow rather than tax-basis profit including noncash depreciation, is a valuable device that appraisers and investors can use to determine whether one property has better cash flow potential than (1) another property or (2) the average property in the current market.

Formula: Profit Margin

$$\frac{C}{I} = P$$

where C = cash flow
      I = effective gross income
      P = profit margin

A related analytical tool is the *breakeven ratio*, which is a calculation of how well the effective gross income of a property will cover cash requirements. If the ratio is below 1.00, the property is estimated to be able to produce net positive cash flow. If the ratio is above 1.00, it will be operating with negative cash flow. However, one also needs to calculate the tax benefits of deducting tax-basis losses, which include depreciation. For individual investors involved with income-producing properties, it is possible to report a tax-basis net loss but still produce a positive cash flow. Two formulas need to be considered in the breakeven analysis: the breakeven ratio (which does not consider the effect of tax reduction) and the breakeven ratio net of taxes (which *does* include a provision for tax advantages). The second formula should be given greater emphasis when the tax benefits of the investment are substantial. For many investors, that defines the difference between positive and negative cash flow.

Formula: Breakeven Ratio

$$\frac{O + M}{G} = R$$

where O = operating expenses
      M = mortgage debt service
      G = effective gross income
      R = breakeven ratio

Formula: Breakeven Ratio Net of Taxes

$$\frac{O + M - [(O + I + D) \times E]}{G} = R$$

where O = operating expenses
      M = mortgage debt service
      I = interest
      D = depreciation
      E = effective tax rate
      G = effective gross income
      R = breakeven ratio net of taxes

VALUATION PRINCIPLES

Appraisers base their opinions of market value on a combination of age and condition, recent sales, income potential (when applicable), and a wide range of other methods for studying valuation. They are further guided by what are known as *principles* of valuation, a group of 10 specific elements that directly affect the supply of and demand for real estate.

These 10 principles are:

1. *Highest and best use.* Property valuation is going to be greatest when land is used in the best possible way. This does not limit valuation to zoning, even though many people think of "highest and best use" as being the same as "zoned." It really refers to maximizing the land uses that are allowed. For example, in a neighborhood zoned for multifamily residential use, building a single-family house may not be the best use, even though it would be allowed under the zoning.

2. *Conformity.* This real estate principle is based on the observation that property appreciation is most likely to occur when the improvements' design, attributes, size, age, and condition are similar to those of other properties in the same area. Thus, an overimproved house is not going to appreciate at the full cost value of improvements; its nonconformity will inhibit appreciation.

3. *Substitution.* This principle is based on the idea that valuation is naturally influenced (and often limited) by the market values of other properties used in a similar manner, of the same size, and with the same attributes.

4. *Progression.* This is the observation that property values tend to grow as a result of proximity to similar properties whose market value is greater. The higher value of properties close by has a positive effect on the value of a lower-priced property.

5. *Regression.* This principle is the opposite of progression. Just as higher-priced homes have an effect, so do lower-priced homes. The principle of regression states that property values are likely to be adversely affected when other properties nearby are of lower market value.

6. *Anticipation*. This principle applies in real estate just as it does in the stock market. This is the principle that states that current market value often reflects expected changes in the immediate future. Expectation has an effect on value, either positive or negative.

7. *Contribution*. This principle states that improvements are going to add value, but in a limited manner. When demand is slow, owners may not expect to realize an increase in market value equal to the value of improvements; when cosmetic repairs are performed on properties in high-demand markets, the opposite effect may be seen: Increases in market value exceed the actual cost of improvements.

8. *Competition*. This is a principle in real estate as well as a fact of economic life. The idea here is that the potential for profits creates competition, and the greater the competition, the lower the market share for each investor. If an investor owned the only house on the market, the price would go up as high as the highest bid, but if 200 houses are built in a town with only 100 households, competition will cause a drastic reduction in market value.

9. *Change*. This is the idea that nothing remains the same forever. Supply and demand interact in particular ways, but the cyclical dynamics change continually. Today's hot market may be very cold next year, and vice versa, and this changes the property values of all properties for sale at any time.

10. *Plottage*. This is the final principle, the observation that consistency in land use tends to maximize land values. Thus, a hodgepodge of zoning and usage would be likely to have a detrimental effect on overall property value, and consistency of use within one area would improve market value. Under the same principle, it is observed that individually owned plots of land tend to increase in value when they are combined under a single owner and used in a consistent manner.

Appraisers face a complex challenge in attempting to place a market value on properties. They depend on recent sales or on comparisons to similar properties producing income in the same manner or to very similar-sized units. Industry standards ensure that professional appraisers in different areas employ the same methodology in setting values on properties. This is a requirement for every investor and lender.

Appraisal and financing of property usually involve someone buying a property outright and obtaining financing for it. In one respect, it is the long-term cost of financing that determines what real estate actually costs, to a greater extent than the appraised value itself. Appraisal is the starting point, in which the current market value is set. What you pay for the property, including interest, is likely to be far higher. Chapter 3 demonstrates why.

YOUR MORTGAGE

THE REAL COST OF BUYING PROPERTY

WHAT DOES A PROPERTY COST? This is one of the most important questions investors ask, and, just as a stock market investor is interested in the price per share, real estate investors need to know how much their investments will require in capital.

This seemingly straightforward question is actually far more complex. Because you will probably be financing a major portion of the total purchase price, your real cost is not the sale price of the property, but the total you pay over many years. Cost has more to do with your interest rate than with the price the seller wants.

For example, a 30-year mortgage is a common device for financing an investment property. If you buy a rental property for $140,000 and make a down payment of $40,000, you will finance the balance of $100,000. If you make payments over 30 years, what is your total cost going to be (assuming you keep the property that long)? If your interest rate is 7.5 percent, the total 30-year payments come to $251,716, so your total cost would be $291,716 with the down payment. That is more than twice the sale price of $140,000.

Now consider the difference it would make if you could get a loan at 6 percent. You would *save* $35,878 over 30 years with this lower interest rate. This significant difference makes the point: You are better off negotiating a small advantage in financing than you are getting a reduced price on the property. A lot of emphasis is placed on getting a bargain; you might be able to whittle an asked price of $140,000 down to $130,000. But if you concentrate on this price difference but fail to shop for the best mortgage deal, it could be a mistake.

This chapter explores the realm of the *real* cost of property, resulting from the effects of compounded interest. The *time value of money* (the value based on how interest compounding affects your cost) is where the real cost of property is to be found. The first step is to calculate how value is accumulated over time with compound interest, as in a savings account. This leads to the *opposite* of accumulation, the payments made on a debt. By coming to understand how present value and sinking fund payments (such as payments on a mortgage loan) work, you gain a deeper understanding of why the cost of borrowing can be so high. For example, you need to be able to calculate present value to figure out important cash flow–based calculations (such as discounted cash flow).

THE TIME VALUE OF MONEY

The long-term effects of small changes in interest rates are important in shopping for a good mortgage deal. You can also drastically reduce the overall cost of interest by making small prepayments on a mortgage. Later in this chapter, the dramatic effects of making extra payments to principal (a process called *mortgage acceleration*) is demonstrated.

Interest calculations show how the amount of interest accumulates over time. Most people are familiar with interest as it relates to a personal savings account. The same effects that you profit from by leaving money in such an account (in which money grows) also works for lenders. Thus, the payments you make on your mortgage reduce the debt only gradually, because most of your payments constitute interest. In fact, a 30-year loan is paid down to one-half only at the end of the 25th year; the remaining half gets paid off in the last five years (based on a 5.75 percent rate or below).

SIMPLE INTEREST

The first calculation is for *simple interest*, which is interest based on the nominal (or stated) rate per year. Three elements are always involved in interest calculations: principal, interest rate, and time. Simple interest is the interest you pay without any compounding.

Formula: Simple Interest

$P \times R = I$

where P = principal
       R = interest rate
       I = interest

This is a straightforward formula. If the principal amount is $1,000 and interest is 4 percent, simple interest is:

$1,000 × 4% = $40.00

In calculating percentages, you can convert the stated percentage of interest to a decimal form, making the multiplication easier. To calculate the decimal equivalent of a percentage, divide the interest by 100.

Formula: Conversion, Percentage to Decimal

$$\frac{R}{100} = D$$

where R = interest rate
      D = decimal equivalent

For example, the interest rate of 4 percent is converted to decimal equivalent using this formula:

4% ÷ 100 = 0.04

COMPOUND INTEREST

It is important to know the calculation for simple interest, even though it is rarely used. It serves as the building block for the more common calculation of *compound interest*. Compounding may occur in many different ways: daily, monthly, quarterly, semiannually, or annually.

Daily compounding can be done in two ways. The number of

days may be 365 (days in the year) or 360. When 360 days are used, every month is assumed to contain 30 days; so the monthly interest would be the same each month, even though the number of days varies. Daily interest is used for some types of savings accounts. The formula used for daily compounding generally uses 365 days.

Formula: Daily Compounding

$$\frac{R}{365} = i$$

where R = annual interest rate
i = daily rate

For example, if the annual rate of 4 percent were compounded daily, the daily rate would be:

0.04 ÷ 365 = 0.0001096

Total interest would next be calculated by adding 1 to the daily rate and multiplying it by itself for the number of days. For example, if you wanted to know the interest for 11 days using a daily rate of 4 percent, the calculation would be:

$(1 + 0.0001096)^{11} = 1.0012063$

Over 11 days, the $1,000 of principal would grow to:

1.0012063 × $1,000.00 = $1,001.21

While the 4 percent daily compounding produces only $1.21 over 11 days, the annual interest would be slightly higher than a simple interest of $40. The compounding would add money to the fund at a higher rate. The calculation of interest on a single deposit is called the *accumulated value of 1*.

Formula: Accumulated Value

$(R + 1)^n \times P = A$

where R = periodic interest rate
n = periods
P = principal amount
A = amount accumulated (principal plus interest)

The *periodic* interest rate is always calculated by dividing the stated annual rate by the number of periods. In the case of daily interest, the periodic rate equals the rate divided by either 365 or 360; the monthly periodic rate is determined by dividing the annual rate by 12; the quarterly rate, by dividing by 4; and the semiannual rate, by dividing by 2.

Formula: Periodic Rate

$$\frac{R}{P} = i$$

where R = annual interest rate
       P = number of periods
       i = periodic interest rate

A process similar to the calculation for daily compounding is involved with *monthly compounding,* but because there are only 12 months in a year, the number of calculations is lower.

Formula: Monthly Compounding

$$\frac{R}{12} = i$$

where R = interest rate
      i = monthly rate

Just as the result of the daily compounding formula produced the daily rate, this formula provides the monthly rate. The same process—using the formula to calculate interest for the number of periods—is used for monthly compounding. For example, if you are working with 4 percent compounded monthly, you calculate the one-month rate as

$$0.04 \div 12 = 0.0033333$$

Next, you add 1 to the monthly factor and raise it exponentially by the number of months involved. For example, to figure a $1,000.00 fund's balance at 4 percent after 5 months compounded monthly, the formula would be:

$$(1 + 0.0033333)^5 = 1.0167780$$

The dollar amount would be

1.0167780 × $1,000.00 = $1,016.78

The annual interest for a full 12 months using this illustration is shown in Table 3.1.

You can see from this example that the monthly compounding of 4 percent interest yields interest at the rate of 4.07411 percent per year because of the compounding effect. This is a small difference, but it accelerates over many years. And that is the primary point to remember about compounding: It accelerates as time goes by.

You can also compute interest on a quarterly basis, with compounding occurring four times per year. This produces a somewhat smaller yield than monthly compounding, because there are fewer periods.

Formula: Quarterly Compounding

$$\frac{R}{4} = i$$

where R = interest rate
i = quarterly rate

Table 3.1. *Monthly Compounding, 1 year.*

Illustration: $1,000 fund, 4 percent compounded monthly

Month	Interest Factor*	Value
		$1,000.00
1	1.0033333	1,003.33
2	1.0066777	1,006.68
3	1.0100333	1,010.03
4	1.0134000	$1,013.40
5	1.0167780	1,016.78
6	1.0201672	1,020.17
7	1.0235677	$1,023.57
8	1.0269796	1,026.98
9	1.0304028	1,030.40
10	1.0338375	$1,033.84
11	1.0372835	1,037.28
12	1.0407411	1,040.74

* $(1 + 0.0033333)^p$

Returning to the example of a 4 percent rate and a $1,000 fund, you would compute the periodic rate by dividing 4 percent by the number of periods:

0.04 ÷ 4 = 0.01 per quarter

The compounded annual rate can be computed for each quarter using these formulas:

First quarter $(1 + 0.0100000)^1 = 1.010000$
Second quarter $(1 + 0.0100000)^2 = 1.020100$
Third quarter $(1 + 0.0100000)^3 = 1.030301$
Fourth quarter $(1 + 0.0100000)^4 = 1.040604$

And to calculate the fund's balance by quarter, based on a $1,000 principal,

First quarter 1.010000 × $1,000.00 = $1,010.00
Second quarter 1.020100 × $1,000.00 = $1,020.10
Third quarter 1.030301 × $1,000.00 = $1,030.30
Fourth quarter 1.040604 × $1,000.00 = $1,040.60

Quarterly compounding of 4 percent results in an annual rate of 4.0604 percent.

Semiannual compounding follows the same pattern, but there are only two periods per year. Thus, the 4 percent rate would be cut in half for each semiannual period, to 0.02 percent:

First half $(1 + 0.0200000)^1 = 1.020000$
Second half $(1 + 0.0200000)^2 = 1.040400$

Formula: Semiannual Compounding

$$\frac{R}{2} = i$$

where R = interest rate
      i = semiannual rate

With only two compounding periods per year, semiannual interest of 4 percent results in an annual rate of 4.04 percent.

The last method of compounding is annual. There is only one period per year, so a single compound period at 4 percent would produce 4.00% per year. However, there is an important distinction to be made. With simple interest, the annual rate would be 4 percent every year, without variation. In the case of annual compounding, subsequent years would see increased interest. The 4 percent rate would be increased based on the once-annual compounding period.

Formula: Annual Compounding

$(R + 1)^y = i$

where R = interest rate
       y = number of years
       i = accumulated interest

For example, annual compounding of 4 percent over three years would result in total interest of:

$(0.04 + 1)^3 = 1.1248640$

And with a beginning balance of $1,000.00, the value would grow at 4 percent over three years to:

Year 1: $1,040.00
Year 2: $1,081.60
Year 3: $1,124.86

The preceding illustrations of compounding assume that a beginning balance of $1,000.00 is being used. You accumulate the value of one amount. So what is called the accumulated value of 1 is a starting point for next calculating the accumulated value of 1 per period. For example, what happens to the calculated interest rate when additional funds are put into the account regularly? This is similar to the way that mortgage payments are made—one payment per month. This discussion begins with a savings illustration to demonstrate how the calculation builds upon the previous examples.

The preceding examples, all concerned with the accumulated value of 1, are useful to show how various compounding methods work with a single payment. However, in many situations, single transactions aren't the norm; you're more likely to make a series of payments over time.

As a mortgage payer, you make payments; but if you were saving, you would want to calculate the future value of a series of deposits—such as money you would accumulate in a savings account over time if you deposited the same amount each month. The formula needs to answer the mathematical question, What will a *series* of deposits be worth after n periods, assuming R interest? You will recall the formula for calculating interest on accumulated value:

$$(R + 1)^n = A$$

In this calculation, R is the interest rate, n is the number of periods, and A is the value after time has passed. You calculate interest on a beginning balance, without change. However, when a series of deposits is involved, you need to figure out the accumulated value per period, and the formula has to take into account the additional funds added in.

Formula: Accumulated Value per Period

$$D \left[\frac{(1 + R)^n - 1}{R} \right] \times P = A$$

where D = periodic deposit amount
       R = periodic interest rate
       n = number of periods
       P = principal
       A = accumulated value of 1

The periodic interest rate is the fractional rate based on the compounding method used. Thus, monthly periodic interest equals one-twelfth of the annual rate, quarterly interest is one-fourth, and semiannual interest is one-half. In this calculation, you are computing the effect of depositing $100 per period into a savings account, rather than working from an unchanging starting balance. The calculation, using the formula shown, would depend on the compounding method. For example, let's assume that the calculation involves three years. That means 36 months, 12 quarters, or 6 semiannual periods. Using 4 percent, the decimal equivalent of these rates would be 0.00333 (monthly), 0.01 (quarterly), and 0.02 (semiannually):

Monthly:

$$\$100 \left(\frac{(1 + 0.00333)^{36} - 1}{0.00333} \right) = \$3,817.93$$

Quarterly

$$\$100 \left(\frac{(1 + 0.01)^{12} - 1}{0.01} \right) = \$1,268.25$$

Semiannually

$$\$100 \left(\frac{(1 + 0.02)^{6} - 1}{0.02} \right) = \$630.81$$

Annually

$$\$100 \left(\frac{(1 + 0.04)^{3} - 1}{0.04} \right) = \$312.16$$

The totals using different compounding methods are different because there are different numbers of periodic deposits as well as different periodic rates. Breaking this down for the three-year period looks like this:

Compounding Method	Number of Periods	Total of Deposits	Interest
Monthly	36	$3,600	$217.93
Quarterly	12	1,200	68.25
Semiannually	6	600	30.81
Annually	3	300	12.16

The effect of compounding is greatly increased with periodic deposits as well as through the compounding method.

PRESENT VALUE: ITS MEANING AND CALCULATIONS

You have just seen how money accumulates with compound interest—for example, how money grows in a savings account if you make deposits over a period. A savings account may begin with modest interest, but over many years, the rate of growth accelerates because you earn "interest on interest"—compound interest. So interest on a single payment into a savings account or on a series of payments can be calculated to determine the future value of an account, using the formulas for accumulated value.

Ultimately, a series of present value calculations is required to figure out how a loan is amortized over many years. The tables of loan payments found in Appendix C make this easier, and you can also make good use of free online mortgage calculators. The following present value exercises are provided to show how the formulas work, in the belief that it is important to understand where these conclusions come from; knowing how long-term interest is calculated is important to every real estate investor.

Present value shows you what happens when you pay money to a lender, or when you need to save money today to arrive at a desired balance in the future. The *present value of 1* is the amount required today to reach a required sum in the future, based on the interest rate and the time involved. You need to understand how this calculation works because it is needed to calculate mortgage payments.

You would use this calculation if you wanted to save up money to use in the future. For example, how much do you need to put in the bank in order to have a desired amount in the future, based on the interest rate and the amount of time involved? Using the present value of 1, you calculate how much you need to save now.

Formula: Present Value

$$\frac{1}{(1 + R)^n} = P$$

where R = periodic interest rate
       n = periods
       P = present value factor

Next, you multiply the present value factor by the amount needed at the end. For example, if you want to save $1,000 by the end of four years, and you expect to earn 3 percent compounded quarterly on a single deposit, how much of a payment do you need to make today? Applying the formula and remembering that the *periodic* rate is one-fourth of 3 percent, or 0.75 percent (decimal equivalent 0.0075, reflecting quarterly compounding), you apply the present value formula:

$$\frac{1}{(1 + 0.0075)^{16}} = 0.8873177$$

You multiply the factor by the desired $1,000 deposit to find out how much you need to save today:

$$0.8873177 \times \$1,000.00 = \$887.32$$

You can prove the accuracy of this formula by multiplying the answer by the quarterly rate, raised exponentially by the number of quarters involved:

$$887.32 \times (1.0075)^{16} = \$1,000.00$$

The next step in this series of calculations is the *sinking fund payment*. As in the previous calculation, you need this step to figure out mortgage payments needed later. A sinking fund is the series of payments that you need if you are to get to a target amount in the future. Returning to the previous example, in which you want to save up a fund worth $1,000 at the end of four years, how much do you need to save each quarter (assuming 3 percent compounded quarterly) to end up with $1,000 at the end of three years?

Formula: Sinking Fund Payments

$$\frac{1}{[(1 + R)^n - 1) \div R} = S$$

where R = periodic interest rate
         n = periods
         S = sinking fund factor

For example, suppose you want to save $1,000 over four years, at 3 percent compounded quarterly. Instead of making a single payment into the account, how much do you need to save each quarter to arrive at the target amount? Applying the formula,

$$\frac{1}{[(1 + 0.0075)^{16} - 1] \div 0.0075} = 0.059059$$

In performing these functions in steps, the first one is the sum of:

$(1.0075^{16}) - 1 = 0.1269921$

Next, you divide the factor by the interest rate:

$0.1269921 \div 0.0075 = 16.93228$

Then you divide 1 by the result to find the factor shown in the formula:

$1 \div 16.93228 = 0.059059$

Finally, you multiply the resulting factor by the desired fund amount:

$0.059059 \times \$1,000 = \$59.06$

If you save $59.06 each quarter for four years at 3 percent compounded quarterly, you will end up with a fund worth $1,000.

The next calculation in this series is called the *present value of 1 per period*. This is the required deposit to be made today, based on an interest rate and compounding method, to make a series of future withdrawals. While this is commonly used in long-term calculations for retirement income, for example, it also applies in real estate applications. For example, let's assume you want to put aside money to make monthly payments of $1,000 per month over the next four months for the combination of insurance and taxes due on a rental property. You will remove money from another account and set it aside for this, but the exact amount needed each month is figured using the present value of 1 per period. How much do you need to put into an account today to have those funds available?

Formula: Present Value per Period

$$\left[1 - \frac{1}{(1 + R)^n} \right] \div R = W$$

where R = periodic interest rate
      n = periods
      W = withdrawal amount

Applying this formula, you further assume that you will earn interest at 6 percent, compounded monthly:

$$\left[1 - \frac{1}{(1 + 0.005)^4} \right] \div 0.005 = 3.95050$$

Multiplying this factor by the required series of $1,000 withdrawals gives:

3.95050 × $1,000 = $3,950.50

You will need to deposit $3,950.50 into an account today to fund withdrawals of $1,000 per month for the next four months. This is an abbreviated and simplified example of how the present value of 1 calculation is performed.

The previous formulas are used as part of the equation for figuring out the required *amortization payment* on a long-term mortgage loan. The formula provides an answer to the question, What amount of equal payments have to be made each period to retire a debt over a specified number of periods, given the rate of interest and the compounding method?

Formula: Amortization Payment

$$B\left(\frac{1}{P^n} \right) = A$$

where B = balance of the loan
      P = present value of 1 per period
      n = number of periods
      A = amount of payment per period

The typical mortgage debt is calculated over a long term, such as 30 years (360 months) with interest computed monthly. Thus, performing this calculation by hand would be exceptionally complex, which is why amortization tables are so useful.

CALCULATING APR

Lenders and investors use specific terminology in discussing interest rates and calculations. These are important because their definitions explain how interest is actually calculated.

The *annual percentage rate (APR)* is confusing to many real estate investors because lenders calculate this in a variety of ways. As a general rule, the APR includes the stated annual rate plus points and other fees that are included in the loan. These fees may include not only points but prepaid interest, loan processing fees, underwriting fees, and private mortgage insurance. Lenders may also include loan application fees and, if applicable, credit life insurance premiums. However, because the calculation varies from lender to lender, you need to first determine which fees a particular institution includes in the APR.

Valuable resource:

Easy-to-use online APR calculators are found at http://www.mortgages-loans-calculators.com/calculator-mortgage-apr.asp and http://mortgages.interest.com/content/calculators/monthly-payment.asp.

The annual percentage rate includes the compounding effects of period interest, as well as additional fees. A distinct calculation is the *actual* percentage rate, which is the annual interest without other fees included. To calculate this, first figure out the periodic interest rate; then multiply the periodic rate by the number of periods in the year. For example, quarterly compounding involves four annual periods and monthly compounding involves 12.

Formula: Actual Percentage Rate

$$\left[\left(\frac{i}{P} \right) + 1 \right]^n - 1 = R$$

where i = annual interest rate
P = number of periods
n = number of periods in a full year
R = periodic interest rate

For example, the actual percentage rate for 6 percent compounded quarterly is:

$$\left[\left(\frac{0.06}{4} \right) + 1 \right]^4 - 1 = 0.061364 \ (6.14\%)$$

Note that the decimal-based total of 0.061364 is converted to percentage form by multiplying the decimal by 100. You can conclude from this that the actual annual interest rate for 6 percent compounded quarterly is 6.14 percent.

The accumulated value and present value calculations are significant because they show you how interest accumulates over time. This explains why it takes 30 years to pay down a loan, and why you end up paying more than twice the loan amount.

The process of paying a loan all the way until it is paid off is called *full amortization*. This is different from other types of loan arrangements. For example, an interest-only arrangement reduces payments but does not pay down any of the loan. Some loans are negotiated with payments equal to full amortization, but with an earlier due date. This requires payment of a balloon or refinancing of the amount borrowed. So there are many different types of mortgage arrangements. When you hear the term *creative financing*, it often means that a lender has devised a way to qualify a borrower; in other cases, it actually means "expensive financing."

WHAT PROPERTY REALLY COSTS

You can easily prove that the real cost of property is far higher than the purchase price. You simply need to check the required payment from a loan amortization schedule and multiply that by the months involved. To calculate the total cost of a loan, add the down payment to the total of payments.

Formula: Cost of Financed Property

$(P \times M) + D = C$

where P = monthly payment
       M = number of months in loan term
       D = down payment
       C = total cost of property

For example, if the price you pay for a property is $150,000 and you make a $50,000 down payment, you finance the balance of $100,000. At 6 percent, your monthly payment will be $599.55 for 30 years, or 360 months. Applying the formula,

($599.55 × 360) + $50,000 = $265,838.00

Lenders may offer a reduced interest rate in exchange for higher down payments. For example, consider the difference it makes if you increase a down payment to $60,000 and finance $90,000 at 5 percent. That reduces the monthly payment to $483.14 and the total cost to:

($483.14 × 360) + $60,000 = $233,930.40

This change reduces the monthly payments by $116.41 and the overall cost by $31,907.60. The savings are even greater when the repayment period is lowered. For example, if you were able to pay off the same $90,000 loan in 25 years instead of 30, the payments would be $526.13 and the total cost would be:

($526.13 × 300) + $60,000 = $217,839.00

LOWERING THE TOTAL COST OF A PROPERTY

The lower the interest rate and the faster the loan is repaid, the lower the overall cost of property. This has to be balanced against the affordability of payments. In addition, you have to be able to qualify for the monthly payment level based on a lender's criteria for approval. This is why many people accept extended loan terms. The lower monthly payment is more expensive, but they cannot qualify for higher payments. In some cases, the overall cost can still be reduced through voluntary accelerated amortization.

For example, let's assume that you have financed $100,000 at 6 percent and your monthly payments are $599.55. By adding $44.75 to each payment, you cut five full years off the repayment term. This also saves $22,548.00 in interest:

$599.55 × 360 months = $215,838.00
$644.30 × 300 months = 193,290.00
     Savings $ 22,548.00

At the point of negotiation with a lender, you may be able to get a reduced interest rate in exchange for other concessions, such as a higher down payment or a shorter repayment term. Reduced rates are also available for variable-rate mortgages, although that includes the uncertainty about future interest costs. Depending on your circumstances and financial condition, any of these negotiation issues—down payment, repayment term, and variable or fixed rates—should all be considered. Offers from competing lenders should also be compared, which is an easier task with online financing.

Valuable resource:

Check and compare available mortgage rates by searching online; check the following sites for mortgage offers and rates:

> http://mortgages.interest.com
> http:/www.bankrate.com
> http:/www.mortgage101.com

Mortgage rates for first mortgages and subsequent mortgages are rarely available at the same interest rate. To calculate the overall rate you are paying when you are carrying two or more mortgages, it is necessary to weight each side according to the debt level. For example, if you have two loans and two different principal amounts, you cannot simply take an average of the two rates.

Suppose you have a first mortgage with a balance of $80,000 and a second mortgage with a balance of at $20,000. The rate on the first mortgage rate is 7.0 percent, and that on the second is 11 percent. To calculate your *average* rate, you need to account for the relative weight of each loan.

Formula: Weighted Average Interest Rate

$$\frac{(L_1 \times R_1) + (L_2 \times R_2)}{L_t} = A$$

where L_1 = balance, loan 1
     L_2 = balance, loan 2
     L_t = total balances of loans
     R_1 = rate on loan 1
     R_2 = rate on loan 2
     A = average interest rate

Applying this formula to the example gives:

$$\frac{(\$80,000 \times 7\%) + (\$20,000 \times 11\%)}{\$100,000} = 7.8\%$$

This disproportionate average is accurate, but the average is far lower than it would be with a straight balanced average of 9 percent (halfway between 7 percent and 11 percent). This is due to the weighting of the loans themselves. The 80/100 in the first mortgage has more weight than the 20/100 in the second mortgage.

The same procedure can be used when three or more loans are in force. For example, assume that there were three loans with the following features:

First mortgage $85,000 balance 7 percent rate
Second mortgage $25,000 balance 11 percent rate
Third mortgage $10,000 balance 14 percent rate

The average rate would then be:

$$\frac{(\$85,000 \times 7\%) + (\$25,000 \times 11\%) + (\$10,000 \times 14\%)}{\$120,000} = 8.4\%$$

You may also need to estimate a payment in some circumstances, based on information you have concerning a higher and a lower rate. For example, if you are quoted a rate of 6.875 percent, how do you find the monthly payment? If your book of mortgage amortization tables includes monthly payments for 6.75 percent and for 7.00 percent, you need to estimate from the available information.

Formula: Estimated Monthly Payment

$$\frac{P_a + P_b}{N} = A$$

where P_a = payment, higher interest rate
    P_b = payment, lower interest rate
    N   = number of rates
    A   = average

For example, your book of amortization tables provides monthly payments on a 30-year, $100,000 loan at 6.75 percent and at 7.00 percent. However, the rate you are seeking is 6.875 percent. Applying the formula,

$$\frac{648.60 + 665.30}{2} = 656.95$$

There are two rates here, one above and one below. Thus, the average between the two is a good estimate of the monthly payment at the rate in between. In situations where you do not know the monthly payment for rates equally spaced above and below, it may be necessary to weight one side to approximate the payment. For example, let's assume that you are quoted a rate of 6.9375 percent, but your book showing mortgage payments contains only quarter-percent rates. Because the rate quoted to you is closer to 7.00 percent, you need to weight the higher payment amount to make the estimate more realistic:

$$\frac{648.60 + 665.30 + 665.30}{3} = 659.73$$

In this example, you double the 7.00 percent payment, then find an average by dividing the sum of the payment amounts by 3. This weighted average provides a reasonable estimate of what you can expect the loan payment to be. Actually, the payment at this rate would be $661.11, only $1.38 higher than the estimate. So the use of averaging is dependable as a method for finding an approximate mortgage cost.

MORTGAGE ANALYSIS

Investors are rarely content to simply find a mortgage for their properties. They are equally concerned with the affordability of mortgage terms, the cash flow that is derived given the level of payments, and the potential for refinancing at lower rates and then locking in those rates.

Most people who own real estate directly are naturally concerned with the health of their cash flow. This is actually of greater and more immediate concern than long-term profits. If cash flow doesn't work out, then investors won't be able to make it to the long term. In addition, it is possible that the cash obligations involved with owning property could offset and even surpass the long-term profit. When you experience *negative cash flow* (a situation where you are spending more than you're bringing in), that is a serious problem. This is true not only because it means that cash in addition to rental income is being spent, but also because it means that the entire investment assumption has not worked out. For example, if you are averaging $600 per month in income but spending $750, that comes out to $1,800 per year, before allowing for unexpected repairs or vacancies. If the property is not increasing in market value by a greater amount than that net outflow, you are losing money. Holding on for the long term does not make sense in these circumstances.

Some investors have tried to solve their cash flow problems by negotiating loan terms with smaller payments. An interest-only loan allows you to make monthly interest payments, with nothing going to principal. If you plan to hold onto a property for only five years or so, this could be a sensible plan. At 6 percent financing, a $100,000, 30-year mortgage falls by only about 7 percent over the first five years, and payments on a $100,000 loan are $599.55 with full amortization. This compares to interest-only payments of $500. So if you are willing to save about $100 per month and, in exchange, forgo paying about $7,000 against the $100,000 mortgage, interest-only could be one alternative.

Another possibility is not as sensible. Some lenders will allow you to pay *less* than the monthly payment required to amortize a loan. For example, in a 6 percent mortgage, you may be able to find a lender who will accept $300 per month as a payment. The problem with this plan is that the balance due rises each month. The $300 is short of the required $500 interest payment, so the loan balance increases, and this problem compounds each month. This *negative amortization* is a dangerous alternative to picking more sensible investments. The investor who accepts a deal like this is hoping that the property's value will surpass the negative movement in the loan, so that the property can be sold at a profit even though the loan balance is rising. In hot real estate markets, this could be possible, but it is a very speculative plan. A hot market can slow down and even flatten out quickly, in which case negative amortization can cause significant losses on the property.

It makes far more sense to approach real estate investing with risk-tolerance levels in mind. Can you afford negative cash flow? If so, for how long? How much money can you afford to spend each month above rents? Even if your estimates demonstrate that rent income should be adequate, what happens if you have a few months of vacancies? All of these questions are basic to the initial analysis of a real estate investment. Leverage—financing the larger portion of your investment—is an important form of risk. This is not to say that real estate is higher-risk than other alternatives. But you should be aware of that risk as part of the investment process.

Investors may employ specific ratios to estimate the cash flow risk in advance, and this is a smart idea. The first calculation is the *loan-to-value* ratio. This is a comparison between the mortgage balance and the value of the property. "Value" is normally the price paid, but it can also be based on the appraised value. This makes sense. For example, if you are making an offer of $120,000 on a property and you plan to finance $84,000, the loan-to-value ratio is 70 percent. However, if that property is appraised at $127,000, the ratio drops to 66 percent. In the sense of leverage risk, the higher appraisal reduces your exposure. Being able to purchase property below its appraised value is a clear benefit, and that benefit is most clearly expressed by a comparison of loan-to-value ratios on different properties.

Formula: Loan-to-Value Ratio

$$\frac{L}{V} = R$$

where L = loan balance
V = value (sales price or appraisal)
R = ratio

The same observation applies when your sales price is higher than the appraised value. For example, if you offer $120,000 and finance $84,000, but the appraised value comes in at $115,000, then the LTV rises to 73 percent. Appraised value that is lower than an offered price may be a deal killer, or (especially in hot markets) it may not matter. The important point is that the LTV ratio is a valuable comparative tool for quantifying leverage risk.

MONTHLY AMORTIZATION

Every long-term mortgage balance drops on a predictable schedule. The longer the term, the more interest expense is involved; and the shorter the loan period, the higher the monthly payment. For example, compare the repayment terms and total costs for various interest rates and loan terms as shown in Table 3.2

The shorter term saves significantly on total mortgage costs at each rate; however, as a practical matter, you will also need to be able to both afford the payment level *and* qualify with the lender. Terms for investors are often stricter than those for homeowners. For example, an investor is often required to make a larger down payment than a homeowner, and the investor may also need to meet stricter qualifying standards. Lenders compare monthly estimated cash flow to existing income and expense levels. They may subtract an assumed vacancy factor from estimated income to reflect cash flow in the most conservative manner possible. So you

Table 3.2.   Loan Amortization Cost Comparisons.

	Interest Rate		
Description	6%	7%	8%
Monthly payment per $100,000:			
15 years	$843.86	$898.83	$955.65
20 years	716.43	775.30	836.44
25 years	644.30	706.78	771.82
30 years	599.55	665.30	733.76
Total cost (for $100,000 loan):			
15 years	$151,895	$161,789	$172,017
20 years	171,943	186,072	200,746
25 years	193,290	212,034	231,545
30 years	215,838	239,508	264,155

have to first find out if you can qualify with a lender—before deciding how (or whether) to pay off a mortgage more rapidly.

Investors need not only to find and qualify for the best possible loan, but also to be able to calculate the monthly breakdowns between principal and interest. Some lenders provide this breakdown for you, but many do not. In order to properly record your mortgage payment in your books each month, you will need to be able to divide the payment between its two major components.

If your payment includes additional impound items (insurance and taxes), these have to be isolated before you perform the loan amortization calculation. So a payment may include two segments: principal/interest and impounds.

Formula: Monthly Loan Amortization

$$PB - \{T - [PB \times (i \div 12)]\} = NB$$

where PB = previous balance, mortgage loan
     T   = total payment
     i   = interest rate
     NB = new balance, mortgage loan

For example, a mortgage loan currently has a balance of $100.000.00, and the interest rate is 6 percent (compounded monthly) with a 30-year term. Monthly payments are $599.55. To apply the formula,

$$\$100{,}000.00 - \{\$599.55 - [\$100{,}000.00 \times (0.06 \div 12)]\}$$
$$= \$99{,}900.45$$

The middle calculation is a computation of interest. Six percent (decimal equivalent 0.06) is divided by 12 to reflect the current month's interest expense, 0.005. That is multiplied by the previous loan balance to calculate this month's interest:

$$\$100{,}000 \times 0.005 = \$500.00$$

The interest for the current month is then deducted from the total payment to calculate this month's principal:

$$\$599.55 - \$500.00 = \$99.55$$

Finally, the current month's principal is deducted from the previous balance to find the loan's new balance:

$100,000.00 − $99.55 = $99,900.45

The same procedure is duplicated each month, as shown in Table 3.3.

Online mortgage calculators

It is valuable to know how to break down a mortgage payment; however, to simplify the task for extended calculations, use one of the many free online mortgage calculators. Check the following lines for examples:

http://mortgages.interest.com/content/calculators/index.asp
http://www.mortgage-calc.com/
http://www.bankrate.com/brm/mortgage-calculator.asp
http://www.bloomberg.com/analysis/calculators/mortgage.html

If you continue to calculate a year's payments by hand, two important math checks should be performed. First is the verifica-

Table 3.3.   Mortgage Amortization, 1 Year.

Example: 6 percent interest, compounded monthly, 30-year term, and $100,000 loan.

Month	Total Payment	Interest	Principal	Loan Balance
				$100,000.00
1	$599.55	$500.00	$99.55	99,900.45
2	599.55	499.50	100.05	99,800.40
3	599.55	499.00	100.55	99,699.85
4	$599.55	$498.50	$101.05	$99,598.80
5	599.55	497.99	101.56	99,497.14
6	599.55	497.49	102.06	99,395.18
7	$599.55	$496.98	$102.57	$99,292.61
8	599.55	496.46	103.09	99,189.52
9	599.55	495.95	103.60	99,085.92
10	$599.55	$495.43	$104.12	$98,981.80
11	599.55	494.91	104.64	98,877.16
12	599.55	494.39	105.16	98,772.00
Total	$7,194.60	$5,966.60	$1,228.00	

tion between interest and principal. The sum of the two should equal the total of payments; if it does not, there is a math error in the calculations.

Formula: Math Check, Interest/Principal

P + I = T

where P = principal amounts
     I = interest amounts
     T = total of payments

For example, in the table, each month's payment was broken down to find the totals for each category. To verify,

$5,966.59 + $1,228.01 = $7,194.60

This is correct. The monthly payments of $599.55 add up to $7,194.60 per year.

The second verification step is to subtract the ending loan balance from the beginning loan balance; the net should be equal to the total principal for the year.

Formula: Math Check, Change in Loan Balance

PB − NB = P

where PB = previous balance, mortgage loan
     NB = new balance, mortgage loan
     P = principal payments

In the case of the calculation performed on the table,

$100,000.00 − $98,771.99 = $1,228.01

This is correct; the sum of the calculated principal payments is $1,228.01.

CASH FLOW CALCULATIONS

The key to deciding whether a real estate investment is sensible is found in cash flow analysis. There are complex models of this analysis, as well as practical and easier ways to make comparative judgments.

One method is called *discounted cash flow* analysis. This is an estimate of the present value of future earnings, meaning what today's cash flow is worth in terms of future profits. The problem with this model is that it is based on two separate models: one for today's present value and the other for assumed earnings into the future. For most individual investors, discounted cash flow is too obscure to be of practical use.

A far more immediate concern is the net cash flow you gain from real estate investments. This has to include calculation of tax benefits for reported losses, because those benefits can be substantial. The actual calculation of cash flow requires certain adjustments, because cash flow is not simply a matter of figuring out rent income and expenses. The following items have to be adjusted:

1. *Mortgage principal payments.* The amount of interest paid each month is an expense, but the principal payments are not. So the portion of payments going to principal do not affect profits, but they do affect cash flow.

2. *Depreciation expense.* Cash expenses affect both profit and cash flow. However, one of the most significant expenses is depreciation, which is calculated based on the value of improvements (such as buildings, for example). While no cash is paid out for depreciation, a deduction is allowed. So depreciation (see Chapter 11) affects profits, but not cash flow.

3. *Capital expenditures.* Any money spent for capital improvements to property, such as major repairs, equipment, and other depreciable assets, (see Chapter 8) affects cash flow, but those expenditures cannot be deducted as expenses.

4. *Effect of reduced income taxes.* If you report a loss on your tax return, your tax liability is reduced. This improves cash flow, so the benefit has to be calculated as part of your after-tax cash flow.

The combined effect of these adjustments is shown in the worksheet in Figure 3.1.

Figure 3.1.   Worksheet for After-Tax Cash Flow.

Worksheet, After-Tax Cash Flow
Date _____

	Profit and Loss	Cash Flow
Rent receipts	————	————
Mortgage principal	( )	( )
Cash expenses	( )	
Depreciation		
Capital expenditures		( )
Net profit or loss	————	
Taxes: Federal		( )
State		( )
Net cash flow		————

TAX EQUATIONS

To calculate each side (profit or loss and cash flow), each of the line items is treated differently.

Formula: After-Tax Cash Flow

$$[R - (E + D)] - [P + C - T] = CF$$

where R = rental income
      E = cash expenses

```
D  = depreciation
P  = principal payments
C  = capital expenditures
T  = income tax savings
CF = after-tax cash flow
```

In this calculation, the reported net loss is used to calculate the reduction in federal and state income taxes. This is based on your *effective tax rate*, which is the rate you pay in taxes based on your taxable income. In addition to the federal rate, you also need to calculate your effective tax rate for state-level income taxes.

Valuable Resource:

To find tax rates and income to include in calculating effective tax rate by state, check http://www.taxadmin.org/fta/rate/ind_inc.html. For additional information on tax rules for specific states, also check http://www.statetaxcentral.com.

To figure the federal and state tax benefit from reported real estate losses, multiply the loss by the effective tax rate; the result is the dollar amount of reduced taxes you gain from reporting the real estate loss.

Formula: Tax Benefits from Reporting Losses

$E \times L = S$

```
where E = effective tax rate
      L = net loss from real estate
      S = savings from reduced taxes
```

The computation of mortgage breakdowns and the true cost of buying property affect cash flow directly. The time value of money—or, more accurately, the time *expense* of money—is perhaps the most important factor to consider when estimating profit and loss. Chapter 4 expands on this idea by exploring a series of specific investment calculations for real estate investors.

INVESTMENT
CALCULATIONS

WHAT IS YOUR YIELD?

THE CALCULATION OF *yield* or *return* can be confusing because there are so many variations on the theme. Return on equity, return on revenue, net return—all of these terms have precise meanings and applications, but they are often erroneously used interchangeably.

Return and yield are really the same thing, but the two terms are sometimes expressed differently. Return is synonymous with *rate of return*, which can be further distinguished as a return on a specific measurement (percentage of investment, equity, or revenue). *Yield* is the annual rate of return on real estate (or some other investment), usually expressed as a percentage. The use of *yield* is often limited to fixed returns, such as the interest income from bonds or certificates of deposit.

While yield and return have the same or a similar meaning, specific calculations use one term or the other. For example, in the bond market, a distinction is made between current yield (actual return on the bond) and nominal yield (the stated yield based on the face value of the bond). Stock market investors use the term *current yield* to mean the yield of dividends based on the current per share value of stock. So for most investors, *yield* has a specific meaning, depending on the market. In contrast, *return* is more fre-

77

quently used to describe a return based on a fixed investment
amount (return on investment) or value (return on equity).

MEASURING THE STATUS OF CASH

In real estate investing, the terms *return* and *yield* have many applications; but the variety of calculations is far more complex and setting or comparing value has many different formats. These include
value calculations used by appraisers, buyers and sellers, accoun-
tants, and market analysts.

Calculations required to evaluate cash flow are invariably of
primary importance. Every real estate investor is concerned with
current and future cash flow. If the numbers don't work out, the
entire investment is in jeopardy, even if the long-term profit potential is strong. You need to ensure that you can make it through the
next 12 months, and that is more urgent that the outcome over the
next 12 years.

PAYBACK RATIO

A starting point is related to the first question investors are likely to
ask: How long will it take to get back my investment from net cash
flow? The *payback ratio* identifies the number of years required for
investors to recapture their original investment, which is usually the
down payment on property.

Formula: Payback Ratio

$$\frac{I}{C} = R$$

where I = investment
       C = net cash flow
       R = payback ratio

For example, if the down payment on an investment was
$30,000 and the annual net cash flow is $3,450 (rents received
minus operating expenses and debt service), the payback ratio is:

$$\frac{\$30{,}000}{\$3{,}450} = 8.7 \text{ years}$$

The payback ratio is an excellent comparative tool. If a particular investment produces a faster payback ratio than another, this is a positive indicator. For example, you may consider purchasing two properties, both available for $150,000. One is a single-family house producing annual net cash flow of $3,450; the other may be a duplex with annual net cash flow of $4,100. If both properties would require a $30,000 down payment, the payback ratio will be different. The house's ratio is 8.7 years, but the duplex's ratio is 7.3 years.

CASH-ON-CASH RETURN

A second cash flow–related calculation is *cash-on-cash return*. This ratio is also called the *equity dividend yield*. This is a return calculation used in pooled programs such as real estate partnerships. Usually limited to evaluation of programs based on projections of the first-year cash flow, the ratio provides a good means of comparative analysis. Limited partnerships and similar programs are concerned with annual cash flow, just as all investors have to be, and they try to raise investment capital by presenting cash flow projections; one method of analyzing and comparing the cash flow risk of different programs is to study the relative health of cash flow. This can be done in two ways: historically and as projected. Historical cash-on-cash return is the actual results reported by a program, and projections are estimates of the future.

Formula: Cash-on-Cash Return

$$\frac{C}{I} = R$$

where C = annual cash flow
      I = cash invested
      R = cash-on-cash return

You can also use cash-on-cash return to compare properties you are thinking of buying directly. Returning to the previous example of the payback period, compare the cash-on-cash return for the two properties, a house and a duplex. Both required a $30,000 down payment. The house produced estimated first-year cash flow of $3,450, and the cash flow for the duplex was $4,100. The cash-on-cash in these properties would be 11.5 percent and 13.7 percent. This confirms what the payback ratio indicated: There was stronger cash flow from the duplex for the same down payment. (Additionally, the duplex, with two tenants, provides some protection in the event of vacancies; it is unlikely that both units would be vacant at the same time, whereas the house's occupancy is either 100 percent or zero.)

Besides providing a comparison of cash-on-cash return between properties, the ratio can also be used to get a sense of how real estate compares to other investments. For example, if you can earn an estimated 7 percent in the stock market compared to 13.7 percent in real estate, it adds to your insight. Owning real estate requires more work, while providing favorable tax advantages; the stock market requires little work once the purchase is made, but there are no tax incentives. So comparisons between dissimilar investments are not easily made; all of the factors have to be considered in the mix, including various forms of risk, levels of capital required, and personal risk tolerance and investing goals.

The *discounted cash flow* calculates the present value of future cash flow proceeds. All present value calculations are based on assumptions about cash flow, so you are dealing with estimates. However, when considering a particular investment, it is useful to calculate discounted cash flow as one of many analytical steps. Refer to Chapter 3 and check the formula for the present value of 1 per period. Using the estimated annual cash flow as the "deposit" amount, the discounted cash flow over a period of years can be estimated with this formula. (The factor needed to multiply your estimated cash flow can also be found in a book of interest tables.) Financial calculators may be used as well, but they usually are available through purchase software only.

RETURN FORMULAS

Calculating *return on investment* can mean many things. Some may prefer calculating the increase in a property's market value as the benchmark of success. This is also the most common method of comparison among properties, regions, and other markets.

In considering realistically how "return" really applies, how-

ever, the real return to an individual also depends on the cash investment. Consider the differences between the *rate of return* and
current yield.

Rate of return is a calculation that is used in different markets
to describe and compare how investments have performed. It is
universally accepted as the ultimate measurement of an investment's success. For example, if you purchase stock at $20 per
share and later sell it for $30, your rate of return is 50 percent
(profit of $10 ÷ $20 original cost). In real estate, the adjusted
purchase price and adjusted sales price of property are used in the
same way; and even for properties that have not sold, current market value is often used as a way of explaining how investments have
performed.

Formula: Rate of Return

$$\frac{V - C}{C} = R$$

where V = current value (or sales price)
        C = original cost or basis
        R = rate of return

For example, an investor may point to today's estimated market
value of a property as $300,000 and compare that to an original
cost of $235,000. The rate of return in this example is computed
by dividing the difference between cost and value by original cost:

$$\frac{\$300,000 - \$235,000}{\$235,000} = 27.66\%$$

To make the calculation reliable (and comparable between different
properties), it is also important to annualize the return. So to make
comparisons valid, be sure to adjust the percentage outcome as it
would have been reflected on a one-year holding period. For example, if a property had been purchased for $235,000 and was worth
$300,000 today, the annualized rate of return over five years would
be:

$$\left(\frac{\$300,000 - \$235,000}{\$235,000}\right) \div 5 = 5.53\%$$

The use of the rate of return formula to calculate the paper profit on real estate is valid. However, in this situation, the details of cash flow and tax benefits over the holding period have not been considered. Thus, rate of return may be viewed as an estimate of how property values have grown; as long as the same exclusions are applied to all properties, there is no problem. As in all cases, comparisons should be done on the same basis.

If you want to look at returns realistically, especially upon the sale of property, then you need to use an annualized basis that accounts for *all* types of income or loss. This *total return* calculation is the dollar amount of net gains from the investment; it includes the net income earned during the period that the property was held on an after-tax basis and capital gains net of income tax liabilities.

This raises an interesting question. Investors can defer their tax liabilities by exchanging income property for new income property. In this case, the tax liability is not eliminated; it is only deferred. So in calculating total return, should you base it on the outcome as completed or on an *as if* basis? That would include a calculation of the federal and state tax liabilities that would be incurred if a tax-deferred exchange had not taken place. It is appropriate to compute the tax liability for two reasons. First, you continue to owe the tax, although it won't be paid until later. Second, to make the calculation comparable to other properties when a tax-deferred gain was not undertaken, you will need to make the two calculations comparable.

Formula: Total Return

$$\frac{CG + I + T}{Y} = R$$

where CG = capital gains
I = total net income
T = net tax benefit (or cost)
Y = years held
R = total return

The calculation of total return may involve several steps. For example, if you purchased property for $105,000 plus closing costs of $1,400, the adjusted basis is $106,400. However, under tax rules, depreciation claimed over the holding period has to be deducted from the basis. For example, if you claimed a total of $14,600 over a five-year period, your basis would be reduced by that amount.

The adjusted sale price consists of the price *minus* the closing costs you paid. For example, if you sold the property for $156,000, but you paid $12,100 in closing costs, the adjusted sales price would be $143,900. You must also calculate federal and state taxes due on the capital gains.

Total return also includes the sum of net income received during the year. This should be the after-tax income including rents minus cash-based expenses and interest. For the purposes of showing the calculation, you are assuming that the five-year net income was $6,200. The overall summary is:

Sales price	$156,000	
Less: closing costs	− 12,100	
Adjusted sales price		$143,900
Purchase price	$105,000	
Plus: closing costs	1,400	
Less: depreciation claimed	− 14,600	
Adjusted net basis		91,800
Capital gain	$ 52,100	
Less: Estimated income taxes on gain:		
Federal, 5%	− 2,605	
State, 1%	− 521	
Plus: Net income, five years	6,200	
Total return (before annualizing)	$ 55,174	

The formula is:

$$\frac{\$52,100 + \$6,200 - \$3,126}{5} = \$11,034$$

Total return is often called *return on investment* or *return on equity*. (see Chapter 1). Total return considers the change in property value as a whole, so under that calculation, "investment" is the same as market value, even though various and different levels of down payment may be involved. The return on equity will vary considerably based on the amount of the down payment, mortgage terms, and interest rate. For example, if you make a minimal down payment and finance property with a 30-year loan and a relatively high interest rate, your equity is going to be minimal. If you make a higher down payment and get a better rate by financing the purchase over 15 or 20 years, your equity will be greater. Equity will also grow at varying rates in different markets depending on local and regional market trends. In a hot market, property values may accelerate in double digits; in very cold markets, values may remain the same or even decline.

With these variables in mind, total return (basing the calculation on changed market values as well as cash flow and tax benefits or consequences) is the most consistent and reliable method for calculating the final outcome of a real estate investment.

That final outcome may be many years away. Thus, most real estate investors may be far more concerned with calculating and comparing annual outcomes based on cash flow as a means of determining investment performance. Stock market investors usually measure performance by price per share; real estate investors face a more complex task. However, some of the calculations used by investors in other markets can be useful.

The *current yield* is used in the bond market or the stock market to describe interest or dividend yield. However, there is an application for real estate as well.

Current yield in the bond market is the percentage derived from dividing annual income (interest) by the basis in the investment. Because bonds can be purchased at a premium or discount from face value, current yield is not the same as *nominal yield,* which is the contractual interest percentage paid on the bond. For example, if a bond is at par, current yield and nominal yield will be identical. A $1,000 bond paying a 3 percent nominal yield will also report a 3 percent current yield. However, if a bond with a face value of $1,000 is selling at 97 ($970), current yield will be 3.093 percent (3% ÷ 97). If the bond is sold at 102 ($1,020), current yield will be 2.941 percent (3% ÷ 102).

Formula: Current Yield (Bond)

$$\frac{NY}{PD} = Y$$

where NY = nominal yield
      PD = premium *or* discount
      Y = current yield

Current yield also applies in the stock market. It is the dividend rate as a percentage of the current stock price. As the stock price changes, so does the current yield. For example, if a stock pays a dividend of $1 per share and the current share price is $35, current yield is 2.857 percent ($1 ÷ $35). If the stock's price rises to $40 per share, current yield changes to 2.500 percent ($1 ÷ $40). If the stock's price falls to $32 per share, current yield is 3.125 percent ($1 ÷ $32).

Formula: Current Yield (Stock)

$$\frac{D}{P} = Y$$

where D = dividend per share
        P = current price per share
        Y = current yield

You can apply the current yield in real estate as well by comparing net operating income to the price paid for the property.

The *discount yield* is another calculation of return that may be useful to real estate investors. It is more commonly used in the bond market. Because bonds may be purchased at a discount from their par value, bond investors like to calculate their discount yield. This involves dividing the discount by the face value. For example, a bond purchased at 97 (a discount of 3) would produce a discount yield of 3 percent. This is different from current yield, in which the stated interest rate is divided by the actual cost of the bond.

Discount yield may be used in real estate when individual properties are purchased at a price below the property's appraised value. If you compare appraised value to a bond's par value, you can make a comparable case for using this formula in real estate. If you want to track the kinds of discounts you are able to get on properties, this could be a useful formula.

Formula: Discount Yield

$$\frac{A - P}{A} = Y$$

where A = appraised value
        P = asked price
        Y = discount yield

For example, suppose you are considering buying two properties. In both cases, the seller has a recent appraisal in hand. (Alter-
natively, you may have made an offer contingent on seeing an appraisal.) On one, the asked price is the same as the appraised value;
on the other, the asked price for the property is $144,000, $6,000
below the $150,000 appraised value, so an offer could be made at
a discount from that value. Applying the formula,

$$\frac{\$150,000 - \$144,000}{\$150,000} = 4.0\%$$

In this example, you earned a 4 percent discount yield by purchasing the property below appraised value. This calculation cannot be
applied in every situation, because market supply and demand conditions, seller attitudes, and availability of appraisals at the time an
offer is made will all inhibit your ability to seek out such bargains.
However, as a means of judging a series of property investments,
this is a worthwhile analysis. It is the equivalent of purchasing
shares of stock below current market value; for example, employees
may be given stock options at a fixed price, which may be exercised
at any time. If and when the market price of the stock rises above
that price, shares can be purchased at a discount. There is no good
reason why real estate investors should not be able to make similar
evaluations of property purchased below appraised value; however,
discount yield is only one of many useful calculations that you can
use to analyze your property portfolio.

INVESTMENT CALCULATIONS

Investors in all markets need to devise a series of calculations in
order to compare outcomes. The success of an investment has to
be measured in a comparative way, either against other similar investments or against a predetermined standard. Because no single
calculation works in every situation, investors use a series of formulas to keep track of their investment profits.

The *equity dividend yield* is a return calculation based on a
comparison between cash flow and original investment. It is important to make this calculation on a consistent basis in order to be

able to track your progress. For example, cash flow should always be computed in the same way; one recommended basis is the net cash flow after calculating tax benefits. And original investment should be computed the same way as well; original down payment is the recommended basis for this calculation. Equity dividend yield can be used to judge properties against one another. For example, one property might produce only a 2 percent average per year, while another provides an equity dividend yield of 8 percent. This calculation can be used as a means for deciding which properties to keep and which to sell, based on this formula:

Formula: Equity Dividend Yield

$$\frac{C}{D} = Y$$

where C = net cash flow
       D = down payment
       Y = equity dividend yield

For example, suppose you own two investment properties. One provides an average annual cash flow of $700 and your original down payment was $30,000; the other produces $500 per year in net cash flow and your original down payment was $10,000. The first property's equity dividend yield is 2.3 percent ($700 ÷ $30,000), and the second property's equity dividend yield is 5.0 percent ($500 ÷ $10,000). Even though the *amount* of cash from the second property is less, the equity dividend yield is far better.

In comparison, *equity return* is a calculation of the rate of return on original investment based on net income plus principal reduction, but not the same thing as return on equity. In some situations, this will be identical to the equity dividend yield; however, when you have also spent money for capital improvements, the two formulas will not produce the same result. Net cash flow (as used in equity dividend yield) is the "net net," the amount of cash after considering all revenue and payments as well as tax benefits. The equity return calculation is a comparison between cash-based net income (plus payments into equity via principal reduction) and original down payment.

Cash-based net income requires a calculation to exclude depreciation. Because depreciation is a major expense but requires no actual cash payment, it is possible and even likely that you will experience positive cash flow while also reporting a net loss for tax purposes. This reported loss is a distortion of the actual outcome caused by depreciation. Thus, the cash income has to add back the expense claimed for depreciation.

Formula: Cash Income

$N + D = C$

where N = net income
      D = depreciation expense
      C = cash income

To calculate equity return, combine cash income (net income plus depreciation) with the year's principal reduction on the mortgage debt, and divide the total by the original investment (down payment). To calculate principal reduction, use one of three methods:

1. If your lender reports the annual status of your loan, deduct the current year's loan balance from the prior year's loan balance.
2. Refer to a remaining balance table (see Appendix D) for the annual percentage of debt remaining, given an interest rate and amortization schedule; calculate the difference from one year to the next.
3. Track the division of payments between interest and principal and add up each year's total principal payments.

Formula: Equity Return

$$\frac{C + P}{D} = R$$

where C = cash income
      P = principal reduction
      D = down payment
      R = equity return

For example, suppose that last year your cash income (net income less depreciation) was $815 and your principal reduction was $1,830. Your original down payment was $30,000. Applying the formula,

$$\frac{\$815 + \$1,830}{\$30,000} = 8.8\%$$

Like the equity dividend yield calculation, equity return is a good indicator of how real estate investments are performing. This is especially true when tracking a particular investment from one year to the next or comparing one property to another. For example, consider the case where one property (on which you made a $30,000 down payment) produced cash income of $500 and principal reduction of $830 last year. On a second property on which you made a $10,000 down payment, your cash income last year was only $150 and you reduced the principal by $700. The first property's equity return was 4.4 percent ($1,330 ÷ $30,000), and the second property's was 8.5 percent ($850 ÷ $10,000). The numbers cannot always be relied upon without calculating the actual relationship. In this example, the first property produced more cash income and principal reduction but had a relatively dismal equity return. The second property's equity return was higher, but the dollar amounts were smaller.

Long-term investors struggle with return calculations because they have to deal with several different factors, including market supply and demand and their own cash flow. A higher down payment improves cash flow because mortgage payments and interest expense are lower, but the higher down payment also distorts the return calculations. Different situations are not always comparable. It makes sense to use returns based on down payment levels solely for comparisons between properties, to track evolving cash flow in one property over time, to evaluate property investments on the basis of the overall market value of the property, or to combine the investment basis (down payment) analysis with the market analysis.

INVESTMENT MODELS

A diligent comparison between different down payment and cash flow scenarios shows that calculating return is a flawed art. With this in mind, some investors like to work from investment models. They develop a series of forecast assumptions and use those assumptions to evaluate actual investment outcomes. For example, *expected return* is a rate you expect to earn from an investment if your capital is left invested. You may expect, for example, that to-day's equity return will be marginal, but that as you pay down the principal, the return will improve as well. So in modeling a return expectation, you would factor in ever-increasing principal reductions over the long term.

One form of investment modeling, called *internal rate of return (IRR)*, is a calculation used by most real estate investors because it takes into account the compounding effect of time. So in calculating the internal rate of return, you would estimate an assumed rate of return, an initial down payment, and annual cash flow. This is a complex formula because it requires a series of compound rate calculations. It is also inaccurate because it varies depending on assumed average interest rate, tax benefits, actual cash flow, and compounding method. Most people who like to use IRR employ software because of the complexity of this modeling calculation. Because there are so many variables involved in the calculation, it is of questionable value in a comparative sense. As with many modeling systems, the outcome depends on the assumptions used; so the reliability of IRR is questionable. At the same time, it is widely used and is one of many ways to calculate future return.

Valuable resource:

The U.S. Department of Energy provides a free sample IRR calculator. Check http://www.rebuild.org/lawson/irr.asp.

CALCULATING AND COMPARING DEBT LEVELS

Much of the typical investor's concern involves real estate debt, because in most situations the majority of a property's market value is financed. Thus, calculating cash flow and cash income returns is important, but investors also need to track and compare debt-related outcomes.

The *debt coverage ratio* is a comparison between net operating income and the total of the mortgage payments. The net operating income is defined as rent revenues less operating expenses. These include insurance, taxes, utilities, maintenance and repairs, landscaping, and any other cash expense you incur related to your investment property. It excludes depreciation and interest on the mortgage debt.

Formula: Debt Coverage Ratio

$$\frac{I}{M} = R$$

where I = net operating income
     M = mortgage payment
     R = debt coverage ratio

The ratio is expressed in factor form. For example, if your mortgage payment is exactly the same as your net operating income, then your debt coverage ratio is 1.00. If your net operating income is $7,176 and your debt service is $5,450, your ratio is 1.32 ($7,176 ÷ $5,450).

The debt coverage ratio can be used to compare cash flow between properties. Lenders use various ratios comparing equity to value, estimated cash flow expected from investment properties compared to your monthly income, and other such comparisons for determining qualification for loans. When their ratios are not met, they will reject a loan application or require a higher down payment. For investors, tracking the relationship between cash flow and debt is essential because the larger portion of the property's market value is financed. So with the high leverage, trends in debt (compared both to current cash flow *and* to growth in the property's market value) may ultimately define profitability.

RULE-OF-THUMB SHORTCUTS

Investors can also use a few math shortcuts to simplify the calculation of interest and rates of return. These rules provide you with methods for fast calculation of how long it takes for values to double or triple, based on assumed rates of return.

For example, you estimate that in your area, real estate values are growing at the rate of 9 percent per year. The question: How long will it take for a property's market value to double, or to triple?

The *rule of 72* is an estimate of how long it takes for an investment to double in value based on an assumed interest rate. If you divide 72 by the interest rate, the result is the number of years required to double the value. Using 9 percent, it will take 8 years to double your value ($72 \div 9$).

Formula: Rule of 72

$$\frac{72}{i} = Y$$

where i = interest rate
       Y = years required to double

To verify the formula, let's assume that you purchase real estate valued at $150,000. Using annual interest only (because you're working with estimates of market value), you can perform a series of calculations:

$150,000 \times (1.09)^8 = \$298,884.40$

This is very close to the $300,000 level that would represent a doubling of value. A similar guideline is the *rule of 69*. This calculation is similar to the rule of 72, but it requires an extra step: Divide 69 by the interest rate and then add 0.35 to the answer. This is slightly more accurate than the rule of 72.

Formula: Rule of 69

$$\frac{69}{i} + 0.35 = Y$$

where i = interest rate
       Y = years required to double

For example, if you apply the formula to the 9 percent example, you find

$$\frac{69}{9\%} + 0.35 = 8.02 \text{ years}$$

A similar formula tells us how long it will take for real estate to triple in value. The rule of 113 is similar to the rule of 72. Divide

113 by the assumed interest rate and you will know how many years you need to hold your property.

Formula: Rule of 113

$$\frac{113}{i} = Y$$

where i = interest rate
     Y = years required to triple

For example, how long will it take for our $150,000 property investment to triple? Applying the formula,

$$\frac{113}{9\%} = 12.56 \text{ years}$$

To check:

$150,000 × (1.09)^{12}	= $421,899.72
Estimate, 0.56 × 9% × $421,899.72	= $ 21,263.75
Total	= $443,163.47

This outcome demonstrate that the rules are estimates only and not entirely accurate. Tripled value would be $450,000, and this calculation shows that you can only approximate the time. But given the approximate nature of the calculation, it provides good information.

The complexity of calculations involving yield and return rests with the fact that so many different methods and assumptions are involved. A good rule to set for yourself is to critically analyze the accuracy of a particular calculation, make sure you use the same assumptions and values each time you compare properties, and look at all of the possible methods: cash flow, cash-based income, and after-tax net return. By following this suggestion, you will be able to establish like-kind analyses of various properties and trends over time.

These types of analyses become critical in *comparative* study, not only between different properties, but also between different ways to get into an investment. Chapter 5 explores one example of this type, the leveraged approach to acquiring property using the lease option.

THE LEASE OPTION

THE LEVERAGED APPROACH

MOST PEOPLE VIEW REAL ESTATE INVESTMENTS with the traditional purchase procedure in mind: Locate a property, make an offer, combine a down payment with financing, and hold the property for the long term. This is the usual method of making real estate investments; but it is not the only method. One creative alternative is the lease option.

THE LEASE OPTION CONTRACT

This strategy has two separate parts. The lease is a rental contract between the current owner and a tenant. The option provides the tenant with the right to purchase the property at some point in the future. The option includes several important provisions:

1. *A specific expiration date.* The option must be exercised by this date; failing that, it expires and becomes worthless.

2. *A fixed price for the property.* The agreement includes a specific purchase price for the property. The option is exercised at that price, regardless of the market value of the property. So if the value rises significantly, the seller is contractually committed to the fixed option price. If the property value does not increase enough, the tenant does not have to exercise the option.

3. *A monthly payment amount and breakdown.* A monthly payment will contain two parts: the payment of rent and payments toward the option. The second part may be a periodic option payment, or it may also apply toward a down payment if and when the option is exercised. The lease option contract breaks down the payment and specifies how much of the total payment will be applied toward the purchase or, if the option is not exercised, returned to the tenant.

4. *A right of assignment.* The tenant has the right to assign the option to another person. For example, instead of purchasing the property, the tenant may decide to sell either the option *or* the property itself.

The lease option is a creative way for tenants (possibly future buyers) to *control* real estate without buying it. This is the ultimate form of leverage. If property values rise, there are several choices the tenant can make.

1. *Exercise.* The first possible outcome is the obvious: exercise of the option. For example, a lease option specified that the tenant could purchase a house for $150,000 within the next two years. Near the end of the option term, the tenant estimates that the property value has risen to about $200,000. By exercising the option, the tenant purchases the house at the fixed price of $150,000, which is $50,000 below the current market value.

2. *Expiration.* If the property value has not risen substantially, the tenant may simply let the option expire. The lease portion may be renegotiated or also allowed to expire, depending on whether the tenant wants to continue living there.

3. *Sale of the option.* Under the right of assignment, the tenant can sell the option to someone else. For example, if the option has fixed the price of the house at $150,000, but it is currently worth $200,000, the option has an added value of $50,000. Upon exercise, the house can be purchased well below current market value. However, if the tenant does not want to actually exercise the option (or may not be in a position to afford the purchase), that lease option can be sold to a third party. Given that it has a value of $50,000 in potential equity, it would be attractive to someone else

at a discount. If the seller were to offer the option to someone for $30,000, for example, it would be a great incentive. If the tenant had lived in the house for two years and paid $1,250 per month in combined lease and option payments, a sale for $30,000 would repay the entire two years' rental cost.

4. *Sale of the property.* The tenant can put the property on the market. How is this possible without actually owning the property? In fact, because the tenant has the right of assignment, it is legal for the tenant to offer the house for sale and to accept an offer, contingent on exercising the option. This strategy is called *contract flipping.* For example, the tenant may advertise the house for sale for $200,000 and accept an offer for $195,000. As part of the closing of the sale, the option is exercised and the tenant realizes a profit on the option of $45,000 (sale price of $195,000 less option value on the house of $150,000), before closing costs and taxes.

5. *Cancellation of the option.* The tenant may want to continue living in the property without selling it and without exercising the option. However, the option has value, and if it is not exercised by the deadline, it will expire worthless. One alternative is to negotiate with the current owner. For example, the tenant may tell the owner, "The property is worth $200,000, and the option provides me the right to acquire it at $150,000. I am willing to cancel the option if you pay me $20,000."

Would the owner accept these terms? It depends on the owner's desires and motivations. At this point, the owner will realize that if a deal is not struck, the tenant will acquire the house in one way or another for $50,000 below current market value. By agreeing to pay $20,000, the owner can get out of the option and retain the right to sell, refinance, or hold the property. The math makes the point:

Current market value	$200,000
Option price for the property	150,000
Potential loss to current owner	$ 50,000
Less: Cancellation cost of option	20,000
Profit	$ 30,000

This illustration provides a view of the option from the buyer's point of view. This example makes the point that the seller also has a point of view about lease options. To the buyer, the risk is that property values will not rise enough to justify exercise; in that event, the option turns out to be an expensive mistake. For the seller, the appreciation in value of the property and the option present a problem. If the seller had anticipated this course of events, it is unlikely that the option would have been entered into. The choice now is to lose $20,000 in order to preserve control over the property that has appreciated by $50,000, or to simply take the $150,000 fixed price and lose the appreciated value.

6. *Renegotiation with the current owner.* The tenant may present a different scenario to the current owner: renegotiation of the lease option. Because the appreciated value of the property gives value to the option, the tenant is in a position to enter into an even better deal. The terms are all negotiable. For example, the tenant may propose "using" the appreciated $50,000 in equity to offset rental costs over a period of time (free rent in exchange for nonexercise of the option). The existing option could also be replaced with a new lease option with changed rent, option payments, exercise date, and exercise price. Given that the property has appreciated in value, the renegotiation could include a *lower* price upon exercise, less cost for a new and extended option, or a combination of terms.

THE LEASE AS A PURCHASE STRATEGY OR SPECULATION

The lease option is one obvious way for potential buyers to control the price of future purchases, a type of contingent strategy. If property values rise, the option is exercised, sold, or renegotiated. If property values do not rise, the tenant has paid expensive rent. The lease option is also a reasonable strategic device for holding onto the right to buy at today's price when the investor expects values to rise, but does not have the funds or credit history to execute a purchase today.

The *lease purchase* is a variation on the lease option idea. Under this type of contract, the tenant agrees to buy the property in the future as part of a landlord-tenant lease agreement. This is in many respects an agreement to buy property with a deferred closing date. An earnest money deposit acts like a down payment, and in most contracts the tenant will forfeit that deposit if the purchase does not go through. The lease purchase includes a fixed price for the property but is not assignable like the lease option. So for a smaller cost, the tenant is able to tie up the property and fix the price, and the seller has a deal that won't close for several months.

A potential buyer may get out of a lease purchase by including one or more contingency clauses. Contingencies usually include items like obtaining financing and approval from a lender, going through property inspections and discovering no hidden flaws, or the sale of another property. If any of these contingencies are not met, the potential buyer has the right to cancel the deal and get a refund of the earnest money. However, contingencies must be legitimate; they cannot be included just as deal killers.

If a lease purchase or lease option is to be used as a deferred purchase strategy, these devices can be used effectively. The risk involved is related to changes in market value. One way to view this risk is to consider the alternative of purchasing property outright. If a sale is completed and property values don't rise, the value as an investment is minimal, so the payments made via earnest money in a lease purchase, or through option payments within a lease option agreement, can be seen as the cost of managing risk.

Another reason people use lease options is purely for speculation. The speculator has no interest in holding onto investment properties for the long term, paying mortgages from cash flow, and benefiting from growth in market value over many years. To the speculator, the lease option is a means of creating quick profits in a highly leveraged way. However, as with speculation in all markets, the potentially higher profits come with a corresponding higher risk. In markets where property values rise quickly, the real estate speculator can use lease options to control many properties that would otherwise be unaffordable. However, today's hot market may change very suddenly, and speculators can just as easily lose money, too.

Here are some guidelines for the use of lease purchase and lease option contracts:

1. *Know what you are trying to accomplish.* Everyone who enters into an agreement of this nature should know the potential risks

as well as the potential profits. There is a tendency to ignore the risks and focus only on the profit potential, and that is not a balanced view of the lease purchase or lease option contract.

2. *Use lease options only when they make sense.* For a tenant in a lease option, the monthly rent payment is going to be higher than straight rent, because part of the payment is for the cost of the option or goes toward a down payment. So monthly budgeting for rent payments has to take into consideration the contractual requirement to keep up with payments. As with any lease, if the tenant defaults, the option will expire immediately and the potential profits will be lost.

3. *Decide on a course of action in various market scenarios.* Do you intend to exercise the option, sell the property, or renegotiate with the current owner? Based on the conditions of the local real estate market, you should decide in advance what you intend to do if the market moves up or remains at or below current price levels.

4. *If you enter a lease option with the intention of exercising, be sure you want the property.* Some investors concentrate on potential profits but forget the all-important step of evaluating the property as a potential investment. Upon exercise of the option, what will the monthly payments be, and how do they compare to market rents? Be sure that the property will also work as a rental investment, in addition to providing potentially attractive option-based profits.

EXERCISING OPTIONS

The great advantage of lease options is the leverage they create. The traditional concept of leverage in real estate—making a relatively small down payment and financing most of the purchase—is, in fact, only a starting point. The lease option enables an investor or speculator to control real estate with no down payment. If the conditions of the lease allow speculators to sublease property, it is conceivable that a number of properties could be 100 percent leveraged using lease option contracts.

The risk in such a plan arises if and when property values do not increase by the time of an option's expiration. However, if the investor has managed to find sublease tenants who pay for the entire cost of the lease *and* the option, there is no financial loss. By diversifying among different areas, it is possible to set up situations in which options could be exercised, sold, assigned, or renegotiated in some cases, with a zero-loss outcome in others. However, this scheme may not be as easy as it sounds; it remains essential that such speculation be accompanied with skillful management, careful tenant selection and supervision, and a clear vision concerning the desired outcomes under various market conditions.

Because leases are very real obligations, there is a natural limit to the number of lease options a speculator will be able to enter into at the same time. In theory, a speculator could commit dozens of properties using subleases and never experience negative cash flow. In practice, the role of landlord is going to involve occasional non-payment of rent, the need to evict deadbeat tenants, and the need to repair damages to property caused by neglectful tenants. The plan to use lease options as a broad strategy for controlling or acquiring properties is limited by practical constraints as well as by limitations on locating financing, lease option deals themselves, and responsible tenants.

For those involved in a number of transactions involving lease options, some calculations are useful in judging the relative value of and profits from option activity. One formula compares the cost of the option to the purchase price of property. This is useful in assessing the true cost of entering into the lease option (from a tenant's point of view) or the profitability of granting options (from the buyer's point of view).

Formula: Option to Exercise Ratio

$$\frac{O}{S} = R$$

where O = option price
       S = sale price upon exercise
       R = ratio

For example, an option is entered between owner and tenant providing that the property's price will be fixed at $150,000 and that the option must be exercised within the next 24 months. Total rent is $1,200 per month, of which $200 is identified as the option cost and $1,000 is rent. Over a two-year period, the option will cost $4,800 ($200 × 24 months). The option to exercise value is

$$\frac{\$4,800}{\$150,000} = 3.2\%$$

Another method for comparing lease options is on the basis of the return generated through exercise. For example, if an option fixes the price of a property at $150,000 and that option costs $4,800, what is the *exercise return*? That depends on the market value at the time of exercise.

Formula: Exercise Return (to Tenant)

$$\frac{O}{M - P} = R$$

where O = option cost
       M = current market value
       P = fixed option price of property
       R = exercise return

For example, if an option on a property with an option price of $150,000 is exercised when the market value is $200,000 and the option cost was $4,800, the exercise return is

$$\frac{\$4,800}{\$200,000 - \$150,000} = 9.6\%$$

This is a *profit* to the tenant and a *cost* to the owner, in one respect. However, the real cost to the owner of the property would be calculated as the net difference between the lost market value and the option premium.

Formula: Exercise Cost (to Owner)

$$\frac{(M - P) - O}{P} = C$$

where M = current market value
      P = fixed option price of the property
      O = option cost
      C = exercise cost

If you look once more at the preceding example and apply this formula, you can view the same outcome from the owner's point of view. This assumes that the fixed option price of the property (P) was considered to be the current value at the time the lease option was signed. In other words, the owner believed at that time that the price was a fair price. The fact that the property increased in value subsequently was a lost opportunity. Applying the formula,

$$\frac{(\$200,000 - \$150,000) - \$4,800}{\$150,000} = 30.1\%$$

Another way to express this outcome from the owner's perspective is: The *cost* of granting the option to the tenant was equal to 30.1 percent of the profit on the property.

The calculation of return and cost are performed before calculation of closing costs or capital gains taxes. Because those are variables based on individual circumstances and locations, these formulas do not attempt to calculate the *net* return or gain. For comparative purposes, preclosing costs and pretax comparisons will be consistent.

TAX RESTRICTIONS WITH LEASE OPTIONS

One consideration in the risk/reward evaluation of lease options is the tax consequences of entering into such a contract. In the straight purchase-and-sale agreement, investors who own real estate are allowed to defer their gains through a like-kind exchange (see Chapter 11). This means that investors may complete a sale and pay taxes later. The provision requires investors to replace the property with like-kind properties (other real estate) that costs at least as much as (or more than) the property being sold.

Other conditions apply as well. A buyer in such an exchange must agree in writing to cooperate with the seller in completing the tax-deferred conditions, and the sale has to be completed within six months from the time a property is found and an offer is made. The specific requirements are explained later. One important point to make now is that tax deferrals are *not* permitted when properties are sold through a lease option agreement.

This restriction may have tax ramifications for some investors. The timing of taxable transactions can be critical. For example, if income in a particular year is going to be taxed at a fairly low rate, generating additional income could result in taxes being assessed at a higher rate. So advance tax planning may enable you to minimize your tax liability, even if that means putting off the taxable closing of a deal until the following year.

Some other considerations apply as well. For the owners of property, the option payments received are treated as ordinary income, probably in the year in which the option is scheduled to expire. Because this is a complex area of taxes, owners should consult with their tax advisers regarding the treatment of option payments from tenants.

For tenants, payment of option costs is probably going to be added into the basis of the property. Tenants generally are not allowed to claim a deduction for unexercised option payments *or* for the option cost upon exercise. It is more likely that those payments will be added to the basis of the property. For example, if a tenant paid $4,800 to fix the price of the property at $150,000, upon exercise the basis would be:

Purchase price	$150,000
Plus: option cost	4,800
Total basis	$154,800

This assumes that the full $4,800 was actually paid. If the option is exercised earlier than the expiration date, the actual payments would be calculated. The basis would be further increased by closing costs the buyer paid.

For those tenants who renegotiate options or assign them to someone else, the net profit on the deal is taxed as ordinary income (usually not as capital gains), with the tax due in the year in which the original option is assigned or replaced.

Once buyers exercise their options, they are free to sell the property, convert it to their own residence, or hold onto it as a rental. All of these decisions have further tax ramifications as well. For example, acquiring a $200,000 property for $150,000 does not allow the new owner to claim higher depreciation. The deduction allowed by law is limited to the *actual* basis of improvements. In the example used in this chapter, the property's total basis (before adjustments) would be $150,000. Of that, the portion assigned to land would not be subject to depreciation; only improvements can be depreciated—at actual cost.

So by using a lease option, the real estate speculator may evolve into a landlord. Whether you fall into that role through the lease option or through the more traditional offer on a property, you will need to master the financial aspects of assessing cash flow and profits, occupancy trends, and taxes. Chapter 6 explores the various rental income analyses that landlords need to master and understand.

RENTAL INCOME

CASH FLOW ESSENTIALS

MANY FORMS OF REAL ESTATE ANALYSIS are aimed at a study of the overall market and the supply and demand factors in specific cities and towns. This is a starting point in the decision to invest in real estate, whether for speculative purposes or as part of a long-term strategy. However, when investors make their decisions to buy and hold, they also need to be able to analyze the health of a property's cash flow, the demand for rentals, and market rent rates. The trends in these areas—as is true of all cyclical investing—do not remain the same forever.

THE BASIC CASH FLOW EQUATION

Cash flow is the key element to analyze in real estate. The basic cash flow equation is most accurately based on calculating the after-tax net difference between revenue and payments. However, the equation should not be limited to the study of cash inflow and outflow. While this is critical, it needs to be reviewed carefully in light of how the investment itself is performing. For example, if your cash-on-cash return (net cash flow as a percentage of your down payment) is only 1 percent per year, is it worth it to continue holding the property?

The answer to this question depends on your estimate of how the property's market value is changing. If values are not growing (or if they are falling), then a 1 percent return on your down payment is not adequate. If you could make three times as much in a certificate of deposit (without the work required to maintain property, deal with tenants, and manage cash flow while carrying a significant debt load), it is valid to ask: Is it worth the aggravation to keep the property? In fact, in comparing risks and profit potential between dissimilar properties, the time commitment, debt service, and aggravation (collectively, your *risk tolerance*) should be a key factor in deciding whether to keep a property for the long term or sell it and invest your capital in a certificate of deposit or a mutual fund or stock that pays a good dividend.

Cash flow is invariably at the center of this decision. Most real estate investors accept the premise that well-chosen real estate will grow in value over time. You also accumulate equity as you gradually pay down a mortgage loan. However, you also need to be able to afford to hold onto the property. If your cash payments exceed your annual income, the investment will be a strain on your personal budget and may even reduce your ability to invest capital in other markets. A related factor is the double effect of taxes and inflation. Later in this chapter, you will find a variation on the concept of *breakeven*—the net return you need from an investment to cover taxes and inflation as a factor in the comparative analysis of investments.

Even those investors who can afford limited negative cash flow should be convinced that (1) the negative situation is temporary, (2) it is caused by market conditions that are going to change in the future, and (3) market values are growing at a faster rate than the after-tax negative outflow. These issues become the key questions for investors who are not meeting their basic cash flow requirements.

Is the situation temporary? Because predictions of the future are unreliable, it may be impossible to identify exactly how temporary a slow market is, in perspective. For example, if today's market is overbuilt with rental units, you may not be able to ensure positive cash flow. How long will this situation continue? That depends on building trends, available financing, employment and demographic trends in the area, and other economic factors. Real estate investors face a dilemma when contending with negative cash flow.

How are market conditions going to change in the near future?
Just as it is impossible to know whether a soft market is temporary (or how long it will take to turn around), it is equally impossible to identify all of the causes of the condition. Thus, identifying how things will change in the future is just as elusive. If you listen to experts, predictions are a popular sport. Whether in real estate, stocks, or the gold market, it is easy to find someone who predicts better times ahead. But how do you quantify these predictions?

Is growth in market value exceeding negative cash flow? The most important question to ask when facing negative cash flow is whether you can afford to keep the property. The condition may be caused by vacancies or simply by market rents falling too low to cover the mortgage payment and other obligations. For example, if you purchased a property for $150,000 and you estimate that its value is growing at an average of 5 percent per year ($7,500), is that adequate to allow you to keep the property? If after-tax cash flow is *negative* by $8,000 per year, you are losing money. Even if your estimate of growth in market value marginally offsets negative cash flow, questions remain: Is your estimate accurate? How long can you afford to continue paying out more than you receive? Given the current market conditions, should you sell the property?

To judge the long-term prospects for rental property, it helps to find indicators that demonstrate a trend. If the trend is positive, you may want to wait out the market; if the trend is negative, it may be better to sell and cut your losses. Some indicators, such as a study of the trends in occupancy rates, will help in making this decision.

OCCUPANCY AND VACANCY RATES

Analysis of how strongly a rental property performs is the best indicator of the market. In studying supply and demand, you need to make a distinction between the property market and the rental market. The *property market* is the demand for property itself, matched against the available supply. You will judge this market primarily through the market value of property. The *rental market* is a reflection of market rents and how they change, and of levels of occupancy for available units. Trends are all-important in both of these markets, of course. Once investors become landlords, their interest in the rental market may become a priority, because cash flow has to work in order for the investment itself to work. Three key trends to watch are:

1. *The trend in the property market in comparison to cash flow.* Are property values rising? The typical investor is initially concerned with this question and is most likely to risk capital only if and when the signs point to strong potential for profits in this market. There would be little incentive to buy property if market trends were soft, and the investor could only hope that future values would catch up or that supply and demand cycles would become strong. Some speculators will buy properties in soft markets if they can get deep discounts, but for typical investors, the preferred method of picking properties is to find strong markets.

The trend in the property market can also be studied objectively in the context of cash flow. The return on an investment cannot be measured looking at only a part of the whole picture. For example, stock investors look for growth in stock prices and dividends. Real estate investors usually seek properties that are in strong cyclical markets *and* that have positive cash flow. Because investors like to make comparisons, the combined growth in market value and current cash flow has to be considered to make real estate a strong choice today. If the estimated profit is marginal, why risk capital? Because real estate investments are highly leveraged (requiring a large amount of debt), the risks are considerable. Those risks are justified only when the potential return makes the decision worthwhile.

2. *Trends in market rates for rents, compared with operating expenses and debt service.* Investors need to know that market rates for rents are going to be high enough to cover operating expenses and debt service. This is not always the case. Rents in some markets cannot support property acquisitions, given typical down payment levels. In markets where property values are exceptionally high, it may prove quite difficult to make the numbers work. Even though

rents tend to be higher in those markets than elsewhere, this does not mean that cash flow will work well.

For example, the residential rental markets in New York City, San Francisco, and Seattle would be very difficult to enter as a first-time investor. Property values are far higher than the national averages. Housing prices may be three to four times higher than the prices of similar properties in the Midwest or in suburban areas. However, market rents may only be two to three times higher than market rents elsewhere. In this situation, investors will have to accept negative cash flow or come up with a higher down payment in order to reduce debt service demands. For most first-time investors, both of these alternatives will be impractical.

3. *Changes over time in occupancy rates.* The trend in the local market that most investors watch continually is the trend in occupancy rates. The *occupancy rate* is the percentage of rentals that are actively rented out. In very strong markets, occupancy may be as high as 98 percent over many months or years. However, that high rate may attract developers; high occupancy means better cash flow, so developers may see this market condition as an opportunity. As a consequence, many more units may be built, and the area may end up with an excess of supply. Given the way the supply and demand cycle works, this causes a softer rental market. Because there now is more supply than demand, occupancy rates tend to fall. So the rental demand cycle is defined in terms of occupancy, and the trends can be observed by following the local occupancy trend.

Formula: Occupancy Rate

$$\frac{O}{T} = R$$

where O = occupied units
      T = total units
      R = occupancy rate

Occupancy can be evaluated on the basis of total units, rooms, or square feet. The appropriate method depends on the type of property. If you are dealing with single-family houses as investment properties, the number of units is the most common and widely used method.

In evaluating local trends, the occupancy rate reflects the conditions in the immediate area. It should not be applied to individual holdings of single-family housing in most instances. However, owners of apartment complexes may apply occupancy rates to judge the market for their particular complex or in comparison to the local market as a whole.

A related trend is the *vacancy rate*. This measures the same trend as occupancy rate, but it counts the number of vacancies instead. There is no particular advantage to using one basis for analysis over the other; both provide information about the same trend. However, a subtle distinction may be observed (again depending on the type of property) with vacancy rate. It may be expressed in terms of number of units, time, or revenue. For example, a three-month vacancy would represent 25 percent of the total year. However, like occupancy rates, vacancy rate analysis usually reflects the trend based on the number of units.

Formula: Vacancy Rate

$$\frac{V}{T} = R$$

where V = vacant units
       T = total units
       R = vacancy rate

FIGURING RENTAL PROPERTY VALUES COMPARATIVELY

Investors normally think of *value* as the market price of property. A house that was worth \$75,000 ten years ago and is worth \$150,000 today has doubled in value. This is a reliable and consistent method for overall market evaluation. However, the value of investment property may also be computed in other ways, designed to provide comparative success in cash flow levels or to determine why and how cash flow varies from one property to another.

For example, an investor may buy two very similar properties in one city. One of the properties produces consistently positive cash flow, while the other is chronically in the red. Why does this occur? Studying property-market value reveals nothing about the rental market. While property and rental markets may tend to move in the same direction, aberrations have to be examined and explained by looking at factors beyond market value.

The types of analyses that look beyond obvious market value are especially useful in the analysis of multiunit investments. A small apartment building (one with between 5 and 20 units, for example) may be difficult to compare to other buildings solely on the basis of market value. In some situations, dissimilar cash flow outcomes may be better understood when analysis is performed on the basis of value per unit or value per square foot.

By determining the *value per unit* for two or more multiunit residential projects, you will be able to develop a means for comparison. When you are considering purchasing multiunit income property, it is likely to be appraised using the income approach. While this provides a useful method for comparing and setting value, judging the efficiency of cash flow can be a more difficult task. For example, you may be considering making an offer on several small apartment buildings. All have different numbers of units and different levels of operating income. It may be very difficult to determine which provides the best cash flow because (1) the asked prices are not the same, (2) total rents, operating expenses, and net operating profit are also different, and (3) mortgage levels and debt service will also vary, depending on which building you select.

In this case, the value per unit provides a dependable means for determining how the numbers break down on a basis that can be reviewed consistently. The "value" in this case means cost in most circumstances; however, the per-unit evaluation may also be performed on the basis of total rents, reported net operating income, or mortgage debt. Any of the financial data may be judged in terms of their relative feasibility when the per-unit method is used. While this may not be entirely definitive (because units with different styles, locations, and sizes may command different market rents), it does provide you with a way to make comparisons that can be quantified in terms of cash flow health. Remembering that the per-unit formula works for a variety of different factors, the value per unit works as the basic formula.

Formula: Value per Unit

$$\frac{C}{U} = V$$

where C = total cost or asked price
      U = number of units
      V = value per unit

For example, suppose you have located three different small apartment buildings and you want to analyze their cash flows. However, because the values of the three buildings are dissimilar, you use the value per unit formula to make your comparison:

Apartment	Asked Price	Units	Value per Unit
1	$327,950	22	$14,907
2	$405,000	27	$15,000
3	$420,000	24	$17,500

The first two buildings are very similar; the value (or, for a potential buyer, the *cost*) per unit is close. However, property 3 is far higher on a per-unit basis. For the owner, this is a positive sign regarding cash flow. However, from the buyer's perspective, this represents a far higher cost. So using these data, you can calculate the *cost per unit* to determine how much a property should cost when compared to other properties. This is a variation on the income approach to appraisal, which is based on gross rents in most applications. In the cost-per-unit evaluation, you do not directly consider gross rents or operating income. You are interested only in deciding whether a property's price is reasonable when compared to the cost of other properties.

These types of comparative data are instructive in your analysis of property. Is it feasible to purchase a property based on its value per unit? How does the unit cost compare to other, similar properties? This analysis is not the same as appraisal analysis, in which questions like age, size and condition become important. It is strictly a comparison between properties without going into *valuation* questions based on economic condition and attributes.

The purpose of this calculation is not so much to set a cost per unit as it is to make an estimated value judgment. For example, the owner of an apartment building may use the cost-per-unit calculation to estimate the value of the building. This is useful information to have in hand to compare to what the appraiser believes. If the appraiser uses the income approach, the appraised value will be based on gross rents, so the level of gross rents that a building can support ultimately has more to do with market value than the cost on a per-unit breakdown. So from a potential buyer's point of view, the calculation may be useful in deciding whether to proceed with the purchasing process, even without an appraisal in hand.

Returning to the previous example, you may conclude that the average value per unit (based on an analysis of the first two buildings) should be approximately $15,000. You can use this information to make a judgment concerning the third building. Applying the formula,

$$\frac{\$360,000}{24} = \$15,000$$

You may conclude that, based on a comparison between this building and other apartment buildings in the area, the building *should* be valued at $360,000. If nothing else, this raises another question: Why is it being sold for $420,000? Some possible explanations will be found in the appraiser's report and may include higher than average rents because of the units' size, condition, age, or location. If rents are higher, then the gross rent multiplier (GRM) will be higher as well.

You may interpret this information in several ways. A higher rent level may represent more efficiency in cash flow and a higher net operating income. It may also represent greater vulnerability if and when market demand falls. For example, if a large portion of the local rental market is made up of college students, several factors will influence rental rates. The higher rent levels may be due to the building's proximity to the main campus, for example. The units may be relatively new compared to those in other buildings; this translates into lower operating costs, but that could change within a few years as a maintenance cycle creates higher operating expenses.

The calculations for value per unit and for cost per unit can be valuable to the prospective buyer because both calculations give you comparisons. The explanations of the variations between buildings might lead to the conclusion that, in fact, the price differences are realistic, given other factors. Or the analysis may provide evidence that a particular building is simply overpriced in comparison to other properties. When you are looking at cash flow as a means for comparing valuation, it helps to study value and cost on a per-unit basis.

A similar analysis can be performed on a square-foot basis, and this may work in many types of property evaluations. While the value and cost per unit are applicable to multiunit residential properties, the *value per square foot* and *cost per square foot* can be used for virtually any type of property. For example, if you are thinking of starting out with single-family houses, you may decide to study the asked prices of several different properties on the basis of condition, age, the neighborhood, and many other standards, *and* by comparing the value and cost per square foot. Buyers tend to develop opinions about properties on the basis of size, but without actually studying the size-versus-price issue in detail. So when you look at two different properties, both selling for $150,000, you need to compare them on some basis. If one has 2,100 square feet and the other has 2,500 square feet, you may tend to believe that the larger home represents a better value.

With this obvious conclusion in mind, you will recognize that analysis on the basis of square feet should serve as a means of comparison, not as the sole means of picking properties. When you see divergence in the value or cost per square foot, you may want to try to identify the underlying reasons. One property may be in need of expensive repairs, while another is not. The age, condition, and location of properties may be more important criteria for selection of an investment property; the square-foot analysis may highlight the need to investigate further.

Some investors simply depend on appraisal value, notably those employing the income approach, to determine the ultimate valuation of investment properties. Others will want to go into substantial detail in evaluating the cost and value of properties based on unit cost, square footage, and similar analyses. A prudent course is most likely to be found somewhere in between these two methods.

While you and your lender depend heavily on professional appraisers and their opinions, some additional elements are likely to affect overall valuation from a landlord's point of view; and some of those features may not even be considered in the appraisal. So your own analysis of a property's features may be useful in picking one property over another. On the other extreme, performing endless tests and employing details down to unit size may be misleading and can cloud judgment. When all is said and done, the ultimate test of investment property comes down to rental rates, demand, and cash flow. It is unlikely that, given similar or identical appraisal values, there will be much difference in market rents between a 400-square foot unit and a 450-square-foot unit.

A related concern that you may want to consider in evaluating investment properties is the difference between value and cost per square foot. Assuming that you purchase a property at its current market value, the two factors—value and cost—should be the same. But these may vary as well. For example, if you are able to acquire property below its appraised market value, cost will actually be lower. If the discount is minor (under 10 percent of market value), the cost per unit is not going to be substantial. This divergence becomes more significant when you have owned property for many years and it has appreciated in value. At that point, the difference between value and cost takes on more importance. For example, if you originally purchased a property for $110,000 and it is worth $330,000 today, cost will be one-third current value. Of course, this will also affect your analysis on a per-unit basis.

The distinctions will become important to you in terms of investment analysis, when you will want to study investment performance based on original cost. Improved market value makes profitability (and cash flow) much more impressive based on cost. At the same time, to evaluate your property on today's market, you may also need to use value per unit types of analysis. This is a useful exercise to ensure that your rental rates conform to current market rates for similar properties. If you slip below market rates, that will also affect property value if and when you want to place the property back on the market.

OPERATING EXPENSES FOR RENTAL PROPERTIES

When an investor makes the decision to purchase a rental property, the questions of value are resolved, at least for the moment. In the investor's view, operational analysis of cash flow becomes far more important. Investors will ask: How is my property investment performing? This is the crucial issue on which the *value* of the investment will ultimately be judged.

The operating expense level is the starting point in comparative cash flow analysis. Some properties have higher operating expenses than others, for several reasons:

- ❏ Higher utility costs

- ❏ Property tax variations between states or counties

- ❏ Varying insurance costs

- ❏ Lender requirements that investors carry private mortgage insurance (PMI) as a condition of granting the loan

- ❏ Higher maintenance levels because of the age of the property

In comparing one property to another, either before closing a sale or after, the *operating expense ratio* reveals the relative demands on cash flow for expenses of all types (except mortgage interest, which is excluded from operating expenses). Typically, operating expenses include the sum of annual insurance (both fire/liability and PMI, if applicable), property taxes, utilities that you pay, repairs, maintenance, and "other" (including such items as bookkeeping, landscaping, supplies, telephone applied to rental activity, and auto or truck expenses).

Formula: Operating Expense Ratio

$$\frac{E}{I} = R$$

where E = operating expenses
     I = rental income
    R = operating expense ratio

The following example demonstrates the value of this formula in making comparisons:

Description	Property 1	Property 2	Property 3
Revenue	$12,450	$11,100	$14,006
Insurance	442	601	635
Property taxes	1,455	1,900	1,766

Utilities	695	807	450
Maintenance	381	1,633	783
Landscaping	0	1,200	676
Other	301	530	74
Total expenses	$ 3,274	$ 6,671	$ 4,384
Net operating income	$ 9,176	$ 4,429	$ 9,622
Operating expense ratio	73.7%	39.9%	68.7%

The cash flow analysis is quite different from this calculation. Items not included here are the total debt service, which includes both interest and principal; any payments for capital improvements; and a reduction for the tax benefits if applicable. The purpose of the operating expense ratio is to enable an investor (or potential investor) to determine how properties compare to one another. This example includes a variation for property 2 that is caused by relatively low rents and exceptionally high expenses (especially for property taxes, maintenance, and landscaping). A scenario such as this could indicate that property 2 is not likely to yield as high a cash flow as the other properties. It may also demonstrate a level of deferred maintenance and other problems that could make this property less attractive as an investment.

Operating expenses do not tell the whole story. This is a useful and revealing comparison, but investors also have to consider the tax advantages of claiming noncash depreciation and potentially reporting a net loss for tax purposes. A useful exercise in evaluating real estate investments is to make comparisons among many different investments on an after-tax basis.

For example, you may have only marginal after-tax cash flow from buying property, but the appreciation in market value may be significant. As long as the rate of growth in market value exceeds the rate of inflation, this could make real estate the strongest-performing investment when all aspects are considered (market value, cash flow, and tax benefits). Comparing the return on real estate with the net return you can earn from stocks, mutual funds, or savings is very helpful in deciding whether to include real estate in your financial plan and, if so, to what degree.

One formula that is very valuable in comparing outcomes between markets is the *breakeven after taxes and inflation*. This calculation estimates the return you need to achieve on an investment just to break even, given assumptions about your tax rate and the current rate of inflation.

Formula: Breakeven After Taxes and Inflation

$$\frac{I}{100 - E} = B$$

where I = inflation rate
  E = effective tax rate
  B = breakeven after taxes and inflation

For example, if you believe that in the coming years, inflation will average 3 percent, you would use that rate as part of this equation. Your effective tax rate is the combined federal and state rates you currently pay on taxable income. For example, if your federal rate is 35 percent and your state rate is 6 percent, your combined effective tax rate is 41 percent. Applying the formula given these values yields

$$\frac{3}{100 - 41} = 5.1\%$$

You will break even at 5.1 percent after inflation and taxes; thus, investments that earn that rate are not profitable, but they do preserve your capital's buying power. If you were to earn a 5.1 percent profit on $20,000, for example:

$20,000 × 5.1% =	$1,020
Less inflation, 3% of $20,000	− 600
Less 41% income taxes	− 418
Net profit	$ 2

Table 6.1 shows the breakeven at various inflation and tax rates.

The various calculations designed to quantify value, spot cash flow trends, or critically evaluate investment return all serve you by providing useful information. There is little solace in knowing that average market prices are rising by 5 percent per year if you are losing an equal amount through negative cash flow. There is no sense in buying property when the total of expenses and payments

Table 6.1.   Breakeven After Taxes and Inflation (in percent).

Tax Rate	Inflation Rate					
	1%	2%	3%	4%	5%	6%
10%	1.1	2.2	3.3	4.4	5.6	6.7
12%	1.1	2.3	3.4	4.5	5.7	6.8
14%	1.2	2.3	3.5	4.7	5.8	7.0
16%	1.2	2.4	3.6	4.8	6.0	7.1
18%	1.2	2.4	3.7	4.9	6.1	7.3
20%	1.3	2.5	3.8	5.0	6.3	7.5
22%	1.3	2.6	3.8	5.1	6.4	7.7
24%	1.3	2.6	3.9	5.3	6.6	7.9
26%	1.4	2.7	4.1	5.4	6.8	8.1
28%	1.4	2.8	4.2	5.6	6.9	8.3
30%	1.4	2.9	4.3	5.7	7.1	8.6
32%	1.5	2.9	4.4	5.9	7.4	8.8
34%	1.5	3.0	4.5	6.1	7.6	9.1
36%	1.6	3.1	4.7	6.3	7.8	9.4
38%	1.6	3.2	4.8	6.5	8.1	9.7
40%	1.7	3.3	5.0	6.7	8.3	10.0
42%	1.7	3.4	5.2	6.9	8.6	10.3
44%	1.8	3.6	5.4	7.1	8.9	10.7
46%	1.9	3.7	5.6	7.4	9.3	11.1
48%	1.9	3.8	5.8	7.7	9.6	11.5

is far higher than market rents. And even the most conservative investor will acknowledge that the double impact of inflation and taxes may outpace even a moderate rate of growth in prices.

The purpose of these calculations is not to indicate automatically when (or if) action is required. For example, a declining rate of occupancy in your city does not mean you have to sell your rental property immediately. However, as part of a larger, longer-term trend, these indicators are useful tools for determining the health of your investments. Just as corporate executives monitor net profit and trends in sales, investors who own or are thinking of buying real estate also need to track operating margins, cash flow, and trends in market value.

The need to track profits and losses applies whether you purchase your own properties directly or work through a pooled investment. Chapter 7 demonstrates how to compare risks and profits in pooled investments and other organized programs for getting into real estate.

CHAPTER 7

INVESTMENT ALTERNATIVES

EQUITY AND DEBT

FOR MANY INDIVIDUAL INVESTORS, there are good reasons to avoid direct investment in real estate. These reasons include:

❑ The large amount of money required for a down payment

❑ The risks associated with the landlord-tenant exchange

❑ The illiquidity of real estate in comparison to stocks or savings

❑ The potential risk resulting from possible changes in cash flow

The individual real estate investor needs to understand and accept these limitations. In so doing, the investor offsets the downside with many positive attributes, including:

❑ Leverage through financing, enabling control over an expensive asset

❑ The ability to fund debt service through rental income

❑ Tax advantages unique to individual real estate investors

❑ Long-term growth potential in a historically safe investment

❑ Control over value through insurance and ongoing maintenance

When you study the equation of positive and negative attributes, you may decide that real estate is appropriate, often in combination with a broader investment portfolio. However, if you decide that you are not able or willing to accept the risks of owning real estate directly, you do have a number of possible alternatives.

EQUITY AND DEBT POSITIONS

All investing can be broadly defined as belonging in one of two camps: equity or debt. This is as true of real estate as it is elsewhere. Well-known examples of equity investments include owning your own home, buying stocks or growth mutual fund shares, or holding investment real estate. In all of these, you have an *equity* position (ownership) in an asset. If your choices are well timed and properly selected, the value of that equity will rise.

Examples of *debt* investments include buying bonds (debt instruments issued by the government or by corporations), buying money-market instruments (such as certificates of deposit), or having a basic savings account. When you put cash into a savings account, you are lending that money to the institution, so this is a debt position. You may also purchase shares in *income mutual funds*, which are given that title because emphasis is placed on income rather than on growth. Income is normally derived from interest paid on bonds that the fund manager buys and holds in the fund's portfolio.

Risk levels also vary between equity and debt investments. For example, corporate bonds have priority over common stock, which means that in the event that a company becomes insolvent, bondholders are repaid before common stockholders receive anything. So this safety is an important feature that appeals to some investors. Conservative individuals may prefer debt investing because of the priority of bonds over common stocks. They may proceed with their investments by buying corporate bonds directly or by investing in shares of income mutual funds. They may also invest in government debt instruments—Treasury bills and bonds—which are considered the safest debt investments available. These obligations are guaranteed by the "full faith and credit of the U.S. government," the best guarantee available to investors.

In real estate, you can select between equity and debt as well, and as in all markets, risk levels and potential profits will vary. An equity position that most people are familiar with is the purchase of a single-family home to be used as a primary residence. In the same manner, individuals may purchase houses, multiunit buildings, or commercial property for investment purposes. The down payment represents an initial equity position, and equity grows from three primary sources:

1. Payments of principal on a mortgage loan

2. Increases in the market value of the property

3. Additional improvements made to the property

Equity positions can also be taken in a variety of programs. In a program, many individual investors invest their money together under common management. The pooled funds are invested in larger real estate projects, such as industrial parks, residential subdivisions, or shopping centers. Each individual investor is promised a portion of the periodic profits and, if and when properties are sold, a share of the capital gain. Programs come in many shapes and sizes; many are traded on the public stock exchanges or can be bought or sold without difficulty. However, some programs do not have a *secondary market* for units in a program, so the only way to dispose of those assets is by accepting a discount.

This type of equity position clearly avoids some of the risks associated with direct ownership of real estate; however, the loss of direct control, tax benefits, and decision-making rights also offset the advantages. Investors who choose to invest in an organized program should be sure that they understand their rights, restrictions, and potential profits and risks before investing. One of the more important tests of an investment is whether shares or units can be traded in, and if so, what is the cost or discount?

Real estate debt investments can also be made through an organized program, and the same caution is advised in selecting a real estate pooled investment or partnership. Debt positions can also be undertaken individually; however, investors need to make sure that they understand the level of risk involved in the *second mortgage* market before lending money to investors. The potential profit is high, but that high profit comes with higher levels of risk as well.

INDIVIDUAL LENDING—THE SECOND MORTGAGE

An individually made real estate debt investment is usually called a second mortgage. This mortgage is called "second" because it is generated later than the first mortgage. But the sequence of events is only one aspect of importance. The terms *first* and *second* also define the priority of payment. If the owner of the property defaults on payments, the holder of the first mortgage gets paid back first; if anything is left over, the second-mortgage holder gets repaid.

In cases where property owners default on their mortgage obligations, it is common for little or no equity to remain in the property. So the risks of writing second mortgages are substantial. While default may occur in only a small number of instances, it is a possibility. The situations in which little or no equity is left come about for a number of reasons:

1. *Overmortgaging of the property.* The granting of a second mortgage may itself cause the zero-equity situation. For example, if a current owner has property worth $150,000 and a $120,000 mortgage, the equity is only $30,000. So if the owner manages to find someone to lend her $25,000, almost all of the equity is gone. The $5,000 that remains would be more than absorbed by closing costs if the owner decided to sell. If the owner cannot afford to keep the property, going into default is one way to solve the problem. In that situation, the first-mortgage lender would be repaid first; the process of foreclosure involves accumulated interest for several months, legal fees, and other costs, so there may be little or nothing remaining for the second-mortgage holder after those fees and costs are paid.

Can the second-mortgage holder file the foreclosure? Yes, but to do so, it will be necessary to come up with enough money to pay off the first mortgage, and in the situation described, it would not be worth much to proceed. Chances are that whoever forecloses, default will end up with a loss to the second-mortgage holder; there is simply not enough equity in the property to give the owner the incentive to keep up payments or to sell.

2. *Lack of maintenance.* Some properties end up with no equity because the owner does not keep up with maintenance. In

other cases, individuals may buy properties without demanding independent inspections and later discover that there are expensive flaws in the property. The owner may even discover that the cost of making the repairs exceeds the level of equity. So just as a $2,000 car is totaled when it is in an accident causing $3,000 in damages, a house may also be "totaled" when needed repairs exceed equity.

In circumstances where properties are simply not kept up, the lack of maintenance will absorb equity in two ways. First, those repairs will have to be made eventually if equity is to be recaptured. Second, as long as the property is kept in an undermaintained condition, its appreciation is not going to keep up with that of other properties, so market value will not continue to grow—at least not at the pace of properly maintained properties in the same area.

3. *Destruction of property by the residents.* It is also possible that the residents of a property will destroy the interior. A home-owner may trash a home; it is more likely that tenants will do damage. While some forms of damage may be covered under a home-owner's insurance policy, other types may not be. If the owner causes damage, no insurance payments will be made. If tenants do damage and owners don't fix that damage (with or without insurance), then equity will drop, possibly to zero in severe cases.

4. *Market conditions.* Finally, equity can disappear from properties as a result of a low-demand market. While this condition is cyclical in many cases, it is not always possible for owners to wait out the market. For example, if a homeowner is carrying a $120,000 first mortgage on a $150,000 home, and also finds an individual investor to grant a $25,000 second mortgage, that leaves only $5,000 in equity. In addition to there being marginal equity, the problem here is that selling the property would cost more than the equity available, so owners would have no incentive to sell; they would not get any cash out of the sale, and they might even have to come up with additional funds to pay the closing costs.

The risk is serious in these circumstances, which is why lenders do not like to see property mortgaged too heavily. Now consider what would happen if property values were to fall. For example, if the property value in this example dropped to $140,000, the owner would have *negative* equity of $5,000 ($145,000 in mortgages minus market value of $140,000). In order to sell, the owner would have to pay that $5,000 shortfall plus all of the seller's closing costs (real estate commission, inspection fees, escrow fees, filing costs, and more). Such fees may end up being as much as $10,000 or even more. So in this situation, the owner cannot afford to sell. The market condition makes default more likely and, from the unfortunate owner's point of view, possibly the best alternative available.

These risks can be mitigated in several ways. Anyone who goes into the second-mortgage market may want to take these six steps:

1. *Limit lending so that owners still have equity.* If you want to be a second-mortgage lender, you may start out by looking for situations where there is considerable equity available in the property. For example, you may work only with people who have equity of 30 percent of current market value or more, and you may further decide that you will never lend money that will take equity below the 20 percent level.

2. *Select possible borrowers carefully.* Whom will you work with? You may limit the potential field of borrowers in several ways. For example, some people work solely with retirement fund managers and offer second mortgages as part of a formal retirement program. Because people deposit funds into such programs and cannot withdraw those funds without penalty, this is a fairly safe venue for second mortgages—especially when an individual's account is professionally managed.

3. *Check credit thoroughly, just as other lenders do.* If you work directly with individuals who want to borrow money, insist on getting a current credit report and ask for a written loan application. Also check out the individual's credit history, current job status, and other important information. Go through the same steps a conventional lender goes through to ensure that the person applying for the loan is likely to maintain a repayment schedule.

4. *Limit the amount of second mortgages.* You can also limit lending risks by placing a ceiling on the amount you are willing to lend through an individual second mortgage. If there is a default, this will limit your losses. For example, you are better off lending $10,000 to each of five different people than you are lending $50,000 to one person.

5. *Lend money only on owner-occupied residential properties.* Risks of default are lowest for owner-occupied homes. People are less likely to default on their own homes than on investment property. So another way to limit risks is by restricting your potential field of borrowers to the lowest-risk individuals: homeowners.

6. *Reduce risk by purchasing second mortgages at a discount.* A variation on the theme of granting second mortgages is *buying* those mortgages from other lenders. For example, a current second-mortgage holder might want to get out of the situation and free up cash to use elsewhere. As a purchaser of second mortgages, you can advertise that you will buy them at a discount. Depending on how badly the current owner wants out, you may be able to get a deep discount—perhaps more than 50 percent—and buy loans at a fraction of the amount owed. In some cases, this strategy involves greater risks: The mortgage holder may believe the debtor is going to default on the loan, so you risk a higher rate of defaults when you buy loans at a discount.

You can also create a second mortgage on a discounted basis when someone wants to get out of an equity position with a co-owner. For example, if someone owns property in joint tenancy and one person wants to leave, that person may be seeking a way to get his equity out of the property. This is difficult if the other person does not want to sell. So in a divorce or a parting of the ways between people who are cohabitating, the situation may be impossible. One person wants her money, and the other does not want to sell. In such a case, a second mortgage can be sought. In this situation, it is quite likely that a discount will be accepted. For example, if the individual's equity is $20,000, you may offer him $15,000. The remaining owner will be obligated to repay the $20,000 loan and also to agree to the terms, and the departing owner will get $15,000. The difference of $5,000 is your discount.

DEBT INVESTING IN POOLED PROGRAMS

In the past, real estate limited partnerships (RELPs) were very popular, primarily because they helped people to avoid paying income taxes. Up until the early 1980s, an individual could deduct multiples of the investment basis. For example, in a 3-to-1 program, an investment of $10,000 created a tax deduction of $30,000. Because tax rates were as high as 50 percent, such tax shelters were popular among people in the higher tax brackets. In this example, a $10,000 investment produced a tax reduction of $15,000 (50 percent of $30,000).

That all changed in the mid-1980s, when new rules were put into effect. Today, investors can never deduct more than the amount they have at risk. For example, if you invest $10,000, the maximum deduction you are allowed to claim is $10,000. The amount at risk is the combination of cash and recourse loans (loans that program sponsors can demand be paid).

Another important change that was made in the 1980s and is still in effect is the passive loss rule. Investors are not allowed to deduct losses from *passive* investment programs. These are defined as any program in which investors do not have daily control. By definition, limited partners are also passive partners. The general partners in such programs make investment decisions, manage the properties, and also tend to earn more profit than limited partners.

Limited partnership equity is very difficult to sell once you go into a program. Ownership of units in a partnership usually ends only when the properties are sold and the whole program is shut down. If you want to sell before that happens, you probably will have to accept a deep discount from the program general partners or from a company that specializes in buying up units from current investors.

Valuable resource:

The American Partnership Board is an online auction site for buyers and sellers of real estate partnership units. Its web site is http://www.ap board.com.

One solution to the liquidity problem of limited partnerships is a variation that trades on public stock exchanges. These *master limited partnerships* may be a combination of several traditional partnership programs, put together to resolve liquidity problems for a large pool of investors.

A real estate partnership can be organized in one of two ways. Some programs have identified the properties the partners intend to buy, and the partnership is formed to raise capital to make that investment. A *blind pool* is a partnership that intends to invest in a range of properties or specific types of property, but does not identify any one property that it will purchase. Cautious investors will purchase units in a blind pool only if they know the track record of the general partners and if the partnership is committed to a time period, after which all holdings will be liquidated and the partners paid off.

For many investors seeking a combination of management, diversification, and liquidity, the partnership alternative is not going to provide a satisfactory outcome. For many investors, the desired liquidity is more likely to be found in mutual funds or the real estate investment trust markets.

THE POOLED INVESTMENT MARKET

The concept of pooled investments has wide appeal. Diversification in real estate is quite difficult for an individual who cannot afford to purchase and manage an array of dissimilar types of property. So alternatives like limited partnerships, real estate exchange-traded funds (ETFs), and other pools solve the problem. At the same time, pooled investments lack the tax advantages found in individually controlled properties, so one of the primary advantages is missing.

Even so, some investors are happy to give up the advantageous tax status of individual ownership to escape the higher market risks of owning property *and* needing to use leverage. The greater risk is the big problem. However, with limited partnerships, the lack of a secondary market is very unappealing, and with mutual funds (other than ETFs), the lack of concentration on real estate does not allow individuals to use those pools to allocate capital.

A solution is found in the *real estate investment trust* (REIT). This is a pooled real estate investment with shares that trade on public stock exchanges. They are entirely liquid, and you are able to move capital in and out. The REIT is a pool organized by a management team to invest in specific types of properties, taking equity or debt positions or a combination of both.

The *equity REIT* is designed to limit activity to equity positions. Most equity REITs carry no debt, so cash flow is simplified for those owning shares. Management pools the capital of many investors to purchase large-scale real estate projects. These may include shopping centers, office and industrial parks, or residential subdivisions, for example. An equity REIT may identify a specific project or a portfolio of projects that it owns or intends to buy; or it may be organized as a blind pool, limiting activity to equity, but without naming or specifying a project.

The *construction REIT* finances the development of projects and takes a debt position. Even though the debt is secured through equity in properties, debt REITs are generally considered to have higher risk than equity REITs. In an equity REIT, fully paid real estate cash flow requires no debt service, so risks are limited to management's handling of tenants, maintenance of properties, and ability to identify strong markets. In comparison, construction REITs can run into trouble if a developer or construction company runs over its budget or does not attract tenants in time to begin making payments.

The *hybrid REIT* is a combination of equity and debt positions. A balance between the two may involve partially funding projects that are owned and under REIT management, or keeping equity and debt positions separate. A specific REIT's management determines its policies, and investors should be sure to understand a REIT's investment and portfolio policies before placing capital in that REIT.

The REIT itself does not report or pay taxes; it is a *conduit* for investors, meaning that all profits are passed on to investors to be reported individually. This is a convenient method for investors, since one of management's tasks is to keep track of reportable profits and losses, capital gains, and interest, and to calculate each investor's share. The REIT's management reports to each investor so that the investor can report the proportionate income or loss on her tax return.

While construction REITs (also called mortgage REITs) may be appealing to some investors, they are not the only way to pool investment capital in a real estate program. In fact, equity and hybrid activity is far more popular in the market. A larger debt market is found in the large secondary-market agencies: the Government

National Mortgage Association (GNMA, or "Ginnie Mae"), the
Federal National Mortgage Association (FNMA, or "Fannie
Mae"), and the Federal Home Loan Mortgage Corporation
(FHLMC, or "Freddie Mac"). These programs and more special-
ized similar ones are operated as independent agencies of the fed-
eral government, and all organize mortgage pools for investors.

Valuable resource:

To check programs for the three government agency programs that organize real estate mortgage pools, check their web sites:

Government National Mortgage Association, http://www.ginniemae
.gov
Federal National Mortgage Association, http://www.fanniemae.com/
index.jhtml
Federal Home Loan Mortgage Corporation, http://www.freddiemac
.com

A mortgage pool works very much like a mutual fund. But instead of building portfolios of stocks or bonds, mortgage pools
contain mortgage debts, usually on single-family homes. Conventional lenders (banks and mortgage companies, for example) un-
derwrite loans to individual borrowers, then sell the debt to one of
the big programs. The original lender continues to service the loan
(collecting monthly payments, collecting impounds, making insurance and tax payments, and responding to customer questions).
However, the debt is picked up by one of the large mortgage agencies.

Mortgages are put together into portfolios based on various
criteria, such as type of property, age of the loan, interest rate, or
dollar amount. These portfolios are then offered to investors in
units of $5,000 or more. Investors are paid an average interest rate
based on the portfolio mix, allowing for the cost of management,
defaults, and other fees and expenses.

Mortgage pools allow individual investors to own shares of first
mortgages, which are secured by equity in the property and are
generally a fairly safe form of debt investment. However, the indi-

vidual does not have to worry about collecting past-due payments, managing debts, or dealing with borrowers. That is all done as part of the service by the agency. For many, a mortgage pool is a convenient and safe method of generating current income in a diversified portfolio, without the headaches or risks associated with granting mortgage loans directly. And because the loans in the portfolio are first mortgages, they are collectively in first position in the event that any one loan in the portfolio goes into default.

IMPORTANT TAX RULES AND LIMITATIONS

One of the most important advantages of direct investment in rental property is the exceptional tax rules. Individual investors can deduct losses. In comparison, investors in passive programs cannot claim deductions; their tax-basis losses have to be carried over and applied against future passive profits or used only when properties are sold.

This has to be included in the overall analysis and comparison between direct ownership of property and pooled investment programs. If you want to escape the need to manage cash flow, tenants, and financing, pooled investments are compelling. But the tax advantages of direct ownership are often among the top reasons for buying rental property directly.

In Chapter 11, you will study the tax rules that apply to the direct ownership of real estate. Here are four rules for investing in pooled programs and partnerships:

1. *Income is taxed as it is earned.* You will earn interest in mortgage REITs or mortgage pool programs, and it is all taxed each year as it is earned. So even if interest is not paid out, the year in which it is earned is when the tax liability occurs. Dividends paid in REIT and partnership programs are taxed in the year in which they are paid or credited to each investor's account. Capital gains are taxed in the year in which property sales are completed, so if a program's management sells right at the end of the year, your capital gains will be taxed in that year, even if the funds are not paid out until the following year.

2. *If earnings are reinvested, the tax liability remains.* Some programs allow you to reinvest your earnings in additional partial shares of ownership. This is usually the case with mutual funds, and it makes a lot of sense to generate compound earnings by leaving funds on deposit. However, you will have a tax liability in the year in which those earnings occur.

3. *Capital gains and annual income are calculated and reported by the program.* One big advantage of investing in managed programs is tax simplicity. You don't have to keep books and records for what can be a complex series of transactions. The management of the REIT, partnership, or mutual fund is responsible for all of that, and each investor receives a year-end summary that lays out each type of earnings. The bottom-line number is reported in the appropriate place on each investor's individual tax return.

4. *Under current tax rules, there are no exclusions or special advantages to investing in pooled programs.* Individually owned property is attractive because losses can be deducted; this is not the case when you are not directly involved in managing the investment. All of the current net income will be fully taxed. This includes interest on debt positions and dividends or net operating income on equity positions. It also includes capital gains when equity positions are closed.

No matter what form your investment programs take, you will have to depend on reliable data, and the types of information you'll require depend on a sound bookkeeping system. Chapter 8 shows you how to create and maintain a simple but effective system, and how to use that system to support the study and analysis of cash flow and profits.

BOOKKEEPING AND
FINANCIAL STATEMENTS

DEBITS, CREDITS, AND MORE

THE REALM OF BOOKKEEPING AND ACCOUNTING is seen as a complex, highly specialized function. While many aspects of bookkeeping may be beyond your interest level and experience, you do need to master the basics in order to know how to track your real estate investments.

The level at which you need to master this is not complex or overly technical. Knowing the basic theory, the key ratios, and types of analysis should be enough. Real estate investors face more bookkeeping complexities than most other investors, because the tax rules are also complicated. In this chapter, you will study the basics of bookkeeping, find the formulas you need to know, identify the minimum of functions you may need to perform on your own (such as balancing your investment bank account), and finally, learn what you should look for on a financial statement.

BASIC RECORD-KEEPING THEORY

Do you keep books and records *only* to verify what you claim on your tax returns? No; in fact, while tax reporting is one of the central reasons for keeping books, investors need much more. They rely on the accuracy of their bookkeeping systems to ensure that their trend analysis and cash flow estimates are based on accurate information.

The technical requirement for keeping books results from the importance of an audit trail and verification. In the accounting industry, *audit trail* is a reference to the bookkeeping system and how transactions can be traced through that system. The *verification* process goes backward from a final number on a financial statement. That final number is likely to be the sum of numerous entries made throughout the year; each individual entry is going to be based on a specific bank deposit, check, cash payment, or journal entry. So the audit trail should enable anyone looking at the last stage—the financial statement—to verify information all the way back to the original *source document*—a receipt, deposit slip, contract, or other proof that (1) the transaction occurred, (2) the amount is correct, and (3) it is a business-related transaction.

The audit trail is summarized in Figure 8.1.

The final step in the process, the financial statements, contain summary information only. The general ledger is the collection point for monthly entries to each account. Journals are an organization of all of the entries of specific types. There are four journal forms:

1. *Receipts journal.* This is the recording point for all money coming into the business. This includes the receipt of rent, loan proceeds, and the capital you invest. The total of each month's receipts is posted to income and cash accounts in the general ledger. The total dollar amount should be equal to bank deposits (or easily reconciled from the journal to bank records).

2. *Disbursements journal.* This is where all payments are recorded. While you should minimize cash transactions in the interest of clarity and consistency, it is often necessary to make some cash payments. As a general rule, this journal summarizes payments made by check, and the total entries each month should be reconciled with bank records. Cash payments are normally recorded through journal entries in the general journal. You can also reimburse yourself for each month's cash payments by writing a check to yourself.

3. *General journal.* This is the book where everything that takes place outside of the checking account is recorded. This includes

Figure 8.1. Audit Trail.

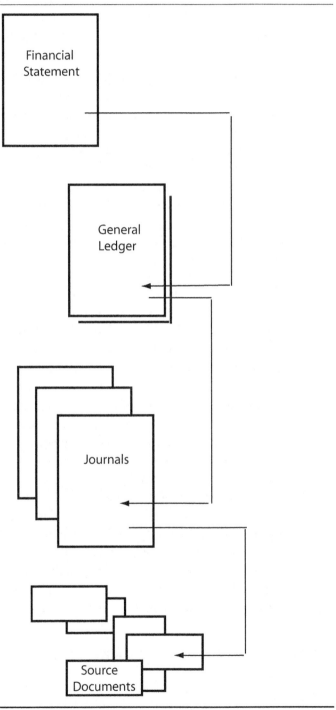

recording depreciation, cash expenses or income, and the breakdown of payments for capital improvements. Every transaction—by cash or otherwise—gets recorded in one of the three journals: receipts, disbursements, and general.

4. *Subsidiary journal.* The fourth type of journal is specialized and is used for special circumstances. The subsidiary journal is a more detailed breakdown of summarized entries occurring in one of the other journals. For example, in businesses that do a large volume of sales on account, an accounts receivable subsidiary journal is set up, with one record per customer. The sum of transactions on account (payments on balances due and new activity) are recorded on each customer card *and* in the other journals in summarized form. The purpose of the subsidiary journal is to manage records efficiently, without making the other journals overly complex.

Source documents are the specific papers on which transactions are based. These are actual verification for every transaction you move through the system. Source documents include rental contracts, which specify how much rent a tenant owes and when it is payable; this supports the rental income you record in your books. Bank deposit receipts should back up the total of the income you report each month, and differences should be clearly explained. Other source documents explain payments made by check or in cash. This includes documents such as invoices, statements, register receipts, and vouchers. In cases where you do not get a receipt, you should write a "note to the file" and provide the date, amount, and business purpose of the expense.

That overview is a summary of what bookkeeping is all about: verification of transactions and management of volume. Note that you may have thousands of source documents and dozens of journal entries. However, you will post a limited number of entries to the general ledger, and that ledger's final monthly balances are the basis for preparation of the financial statements.

DOUBLE-ENTRY BOOKKEEPING

The entire bookkeeping process is based on the concept that anything claimed or reported on a financial statement or on a tax return needs to be verifiable through a methodical and consistent recording system.

Today, most small businesses have automated their bookkeeping system. They simply enter transactions in a QuickBooks system, for example, and the system generates a number of reports: financial statements, checks, deposit summaries, and specialized views of income and expenses for each property. The modern automated system is quite flexible and easy to use, making manual bookkeeping systems obsolete in many situations.

Even so, some people continue to record investment revenue and expense manually. Some have a very informal system, and as long as that works, it meets the need. If you run all transactions through a bank account used *only* for investment activity, and if you label all deposits and checks accurately, an entire reporting system can be based exclusively on your checkbook. You can deliver the checkbook to your bookkeeper or accountant, and a set of books can be constructed from those records.

Some people prefer a more formalized manual system based on the *double-entry system*. This is a system in which two entries are made for every transaction, without exception. It is a procedure for ensuring mathematical accuracy in a bookkeeping record. Every entry will consist of a left-sided *debit* and a right-sided *credit*. Neither of these is more important or more significant than the other. The sum of debits and credits should always be equal, because an entry on each side is made for every transaction. So when you add up the net balances of all accounts, those with debit values should be equal to those with credit values.

The basic double-entry formula is just that simple. The sum of all debits is equal to the sum of all credits. So the net sum of all accounts in the general ledger should always be zero. If it is not, a math error has been made. This is where the "checks and balances" of the system become valuable. You cannot consider the bookkeeping task complete until you balance. This means that you have verified all posting and the zero net total has been achieved.

Formula: Double-Entry Bookkeeping, Basic Formula

$$D = C$$

where D = balance of all debit-balance accounts
      C = balance of all credit-balance accounts

Bookkeepers verify balances in a way that also isolates the net profit or loss at the end of the month. If all debits and credits are posted correctly, and if the addition and subtraction is accurate in every account, the sum of all accounts will equal zero. However, if a bookkeeper adds up all of the balance sheet accounts (assets, liabilities, net worth) and finds a subtotal, that is the current month's profit or loss. It should be equal to a second subtotal, that of all accounts summarizing revenue, costs, and expenses.

Formula: Trial Balance

$$(A - L - N) = P = (R - C - E)$$

where A = Asset account balances
      L = Liability account balances
      N = Net worth account balances
      P = Profit (or loss)
      R = Revenue account balances
      C = Cost account balances
      E = Expense account balances

Note that this three-part equation summarizes the trial balance rule: "Balance sheet account balances *equals* profit or loss *equals* revenue/cost/expense account balances." The format of the trial balance—usually performed in a manual bookkeeping system as a month-end worksheet—is shown in Figure 8.2.

This illustration demonstrates the isolation of the profit for the period. Mathematically, the two "net" values have to be equal if the books are in balance (because the difference between all debit and credit accounts has to be zero).

The trial balance is not necessary in fully automated bookkeeping systems. However, to fully understand how the double-entry system works, you also need to understand the basic ritual of the trial balance as proof of the accuracy of account posting.

THE BALANCE SHEET

The traditional reporting for businesses involves two primary financial statements. The *balance sheet* is a summary of the values of asset, liability, and net worth accounts as of a specific date. That date is normally the end of a year, quarter, or month. The *income*

Figure 8.2. Trial Balance.

		Debit	Credit
Assets:		xxx	
Liabilities:			xxx
Net Worth:			xxx
	Subtotal	xxx	xxx
	Net		xxx
Revenue:			xxx
Costs and Expenses:		xxx	
	Subtotal	xxx	xxx
	Net	xxx	

statement is normally prepared as of the same date and summarizes the total activity during a period of time ending on that date.

The balance sheet is so named for two reasons. First, it is a summary of all the balances in asset, liability, and net worth accounts. Second, it has to "balance" in two respects. First is the requirement that all accounts have been posted accurately and checked. Second, the sum of all assets is the top portion of the report. It has to equal the sum of all liability and net worth accounts. Assets are the properties of a business or investment program (cash, accounts receivable, real estate). Liabilities are the debts (accounts payable, mortgage balances). Net worth is the current value of the venture, including original capital invested plus profit (or minus loss).

Formula: Balance Sheet

$A = L + N$

where A = assets
      L = liabilities
      N = net worth

The various accounts are broken down into subclassifications:

Current assets are assets that are in the form of cash or that can be converted to cash within one year (such as accounts receivable, for example).

Long-term assets are capital assets that you hold. These include real estate, autos or trucks, landscaping equipment, and improvements made to properties. The sum of these values is always based on the original purchase price, and accumulated depreciation (the sum of depreciation expenses for all current and past years) is deducted from these values to arrive at the net asset value on the balance sheet.

Other assets include items like prepaid insurance or property taxes or the value of amortization not yet written off. (For example, when you pay points to acquire a mortgage loan, the points have to be amortized over the period of the loan. So for a 30-year loan, you would record points under other assets and expense 1/30 per year.)

Current liabilities is the sum of all liabilities you expect to pay within the next 12 months. This includes all current accounts you owe (utilities, insurance, auto and truck expense, for example) *and* 12 months' payments on mortgage loans.

Long-term liabilities includes all debts owed beyond the next 12 months, such as the debt for mortgage loans above the current portion.

Net worth is the difference between all assets and all liabilities. It consists of your original capital investment, plus profits or minus losses.

The distinction between *current* and *long-term* is a crucial one in accounting and in investment analysis, especially for real estate investors. The net difference between current assets and current liabilities is called *working capital*, and this serves as a trend ratio used by all financial analysts, in and out of real estate.

Formula: Working Capital

$A - L = W$

where A = current assets
      L = current liabilities
      W = working capital

The definition of working capital is the amount of funds available to continue operating the business (or investment) in the immediate future. So tracking working capital over time is one calculation performed by financial analysts to judge cash flow over a period of time, or to compare relative working capital strength among two or more different projects.

A second method used to track working capital is called the *current ratio*. This is a mathematical comparison between current assets and current liabilities, or an alternative to the working capital formula. As a general rule, an investment's overall health is considered reasonable when the current ratio is at or above 2 to 1.

Formula: Current Ratio

$$\frac{A}{L} = R$$

where A = current assets
      L = current liabilities
      R = current ratio

The working capital formula produces an amount, and the current ratio provides a factor. The factor is easier to track over time than the amount, and the current ratio is universally recognized as a basic standard for judging the health of working capital. Given the special nature of real estate investing, the 2-to-1 basis used for most business operations may not be fully applicable. For many, the ratio is a useful tool to augment the test of after-tax cash flow.

THE INCOME STATEMENT

While the balance sheet reports the ending *balance* of asset and liability accounts, the income statement reports activity over a period of time—a year, quarter, or month. The two statements are usually published together, and the date should be identical (the ending date for the balance sheet and a period ending *on* the same date for the income statement).

The income statement reports all revenue, costs, and expenses of the investment activity for the identified period. It is most useful to show the income statement on a *comparative* basis. There are two versions of this format. The first is a comparison from one period to the next; for example, all rental activity is reported both for the latest year and for the year before. The second is a comparison among properties; for example, if you own three rental properties, a useful comparative format is to show the full results *and* those results broken down for each of the three properties as well.

Formula: Income Statement

R − (C + E) = N

where R = revenues
       C = costs
       E = general expenses
       N = net profit or loss

A distinction is being made here between *costs* and *expenses*. In many businesses, this is significant because costs are directly related to revenues, whereas expenses tend not to vary as revenues grow. So an analysis based on the relationship between costs and revenues is meaningful, and so is a study of expense levels and revenues.

In real estate, costs and expenses are normally lumped together as "operating expenses." That is appropriate. The titles of accounts are not as important as how they are treated in an analysis of cash flow and profits. Costs and general expenses are differentiated in traditional accounting, so both are included in the formula.

Net profit is a key number for investors. It can be expressed as a percentage of revenues, a very popular and commonly used way to judge the results of an investment. While comparisons between net profit and original investment are also made, this can be problematical in real estate. What is your "original investment"? Is it the amount of the cash down payment, the purchase price of property, or the purchase price plus improvements? There are so many bases on which to define *investment* that net profit comparisons are not as revealing as alternative calculations. Specifically, investors tend to be interested in the year-to-year net profit from real estate—the return on revenues, or on income—and more concerned about return on investment when properties are sold.

Formula: Return on Rental Income

$$\frac{N}{I} = R$$

where N = net profit
   I = rental gross income (revenues)
   R = return on rental income

BANK ACCOUNT RECONCILIATION

In addition to the need to keep records and draw up financial reports (for tax reporting, for lenders, and simply to track cash flow and profits), it is also necessary to update and maintain an investment checking account. Operating rental income is the same as the revenues of any small business; it involves numerous transactions each month, and these should be managed in their own account. This is true for three reasons:

1. *It is required by the tax regulations.* Any time you report income and expenses other than a salary, you are required to set up and maintain a separate accounting system. This can exist in many forms, but essentially you are required to be able to separate noninvestment activity from investment activity, and to verify any deductions that you claim.

2. *Separate checking accounts are convenient for record keeping.* The isolation of all deposits and checks related to your rental properties is simple, but it essentially meets the required "separate records" requirement. If you ensure that all deposits can be reconciled to the number you report as income, and that all payments are also business-related, then you avoid having to create the separate records in other ways. The separate account is a great convenience.

3. *It enables you to track and manage your investment cash flow.* The separate account used specifically for rental revenues and payments creates an isolated cash flow. When you simply run investments through your personal account, you can easily lose track of the minor investment expenses that add up over time. Items like payments to a locksmith, a replacement plumbing part, repairs to a window screen, and getting a lawnmower's blades sharpened—in other words, a lot of minor expenses—are constants in real estate management. While these are minor individually, they add up over time. Paying these from a separate account gives you a clear view of what it is costing you to manage your investment properties.

Reconciling your checking account is part of the routine of having the separation. This enables you to tie deposits into the account directly to the income you report for tax purposes, and also to tie payments to your claimed expenses and mortgage payments. So as a matter of sound bookkeeping, maintaining a complete record—including finding and fixing errors—makes the whole idea work. It also requires you to keep the books up to date.

The process of reconciling the bank statement to your checkbook records is primarily going to involve two elements: finding and fixing errors, and accounting for *timing differences*. A timing difference is simply the outstanding checks or deposits in transit at the time the bank statement is issued. It is possible that a number of checks written in the two or three days before the bank's cut-off date will not have been presented for payment, so the bank records will not yet show them as transactions.

Errors can consist of any number of items: bank errors in the check or deposit amount or in posting a transaction to your account that belongs to someone else, simple math errors on your part, or tenant payments returned for insufficient funds are examples. The reconciliation process includes three important steps. The first is finding and identifying the errors. Second, the math in the checkbook has to be fixed. (For example, if you had a math error during the month, you need to correct your current balance.) Third, if the error is the fault of your bank, you need to follow through and have the bank fix it.

The bank reconciliation can be performed using either of two methods. The first method is identifying the true balance by listing errors and timing differences in two columns. The second, and more formal, method is a precise reconciliation of deposits and checks separately.

Formula: Bank Reconciliation

$$(C +(-)E) = A = (B + T - O +(-)E)$$

where C = checkbook balance
       E = errors
       A = reconciled balance
       B = bank statement balance
       T = deposits in transit
       O = outstanding checks

In this formula, you assign the corrections to the appropriate side of the equation. The reconciled account balance (*A*) reflects potential errors and timing differences on both sides. For example, you may find math errors in your checkbook in addition to a deposit you made near the end of the month and several checks you wrote that were not yet shown by the bank. The error should be listed as an adjustment to your checkbook balance, *and* that adjustment should also be entered in your checkbook running balance column. The timing differences—deposits not yet recorded by the bank and outstanding checks—change the bank statement balance.

The process of reconciling your account using this method involves changing the balance on each side by listing the changes, as shown in Figure 8.3.

The monthly bank statement normally includes space on the reverse for listing these corrections. Maintaining a list of outstanding checks aids in the completion of next month's bank reconcilia-

Figure 8.3.   Bank Reconciliation Worksheet.

Bank Reconciliation

Month _____

	Bank	Checkbook
Balance	_____	_____
Plus: Deposits in transit	_____	
Less: Outstanding checks	_____	
Errors:		
_____	_____	_____
_____	_____	_____
_____	_____	_____
Adjusted balance	_____	_____

tion. That process begins by comparing the checks on the bank statement to those checks listed the previous month as outstanding.

An alternative method isolates the area of timing differences or errors by separating out the deposits and checks. This procedure is summarized in Figure 8.4.

The advantages of this format are twofold. First, you can more easily isolate the source of any out-of-balance conditions by summarizing deposits and checks separately. Second, this format

Figure 8.4.   *Bank Reconciliation, Expanded Format.*

Bank Reconciliation

Month _____

	Deposits		Checks	
	Bank	Checkbook	Bank	Checkbook
Total as shown	____	____	____	____
Deposits in transit	____			
Outstanding checks		____		
Errors:				
	____	____	____	____
	____	____	____	____
	____	____	____	____
Totals as adjusted	▬▬	▬▬	▬▬	▬▬

Summary:

Beginning balance	_____	_____
Deposits	_____	_____
Checks	_____	_____
Ending balance	▬▬▬▬	▬▬▬▬

makes it easier to tie the deposits to rental income and the checks to reported expenses.

The format you choose depends on (1) how accurately you keep records, (2) how well you are able to track deposits and checks between the bank statement and your account, and (3) how diligently you want to maintain records. One idea that reduces the likelihood of errors is to double-check every transaction using a simple reverse math process. When you subtract a check from the previous balance and find your new balance, double-check by adding the check's total to the new balance and making sure that equals the previous balance.

For example, suppose your previous balance was $1,335.85 and today you wrote a check for $17.99. Your new balance is $1,317.86. Verify this by doing the reverse math: $1,317.86 + $17.99 = $1,335.85. Do the reverse with deposits: You add the deposit to the previous balance, so to verify, you begin with the new balance and *subtract* the deposit to make sure the answer agrees with your previous balance. You can perform this easy test for a series of transactions. The original math requires that you add deposits and subtract checks. To verify, begin with your latest balance, then add checks and subtract deposits. If the answer agrees with the old balance, your math was correct. If it does not agree, find the error and make corrections.

Formula: Checking Account Math Verification

$$E + C - D = P$$

where E = ending balance
      C = checks
      D = deposits
      P = previous balance

FINANCIAL STATEMENT PREPARATION AND ANALYSIS

Maintaining a checking account is an integral part of the complete bookkeeping system. This is true not only for the purpose of keeping accurate records, but also for reliable tracking of cash flow, recording of expenses and payments, and ensuring that you know exactly how much money is in your account.

The degree to which you keep your books and records accurate and up-to-date determines the reliability of your financial statements as well. Your cash account as well as other accounts should be verified and complete for tax reporting, for your own cash flow forecasting, and for information you provide to lenders.

When you fill out a loan application, you are asked to list all of your properties (assets) and debts (liabilities), and the difference between these two is your estimated net worth. This is a variation on the balance sheet that is designed to demonstrate to the bank that you have adequate net worth to qualify for the loan. You are also required to list your sources of income and your ongoing obligations (mortgage payments, insurance, taxes, utilities, and other expenses—not only on your home, but also on any other investment properties). With this information, the lender is able to make a determination about your likely cash flow and financial reserves. This ultimately determines whether or not a loan will be approved.

In looking over someone else's financial information, you also need to know what to look for. Just as a lender reviews a loan applicant's information critically, you also need to know how to judge a property's potential cash flow and profit. So even the basic decision to purchase a property as a rental depends on your ability to make sound judgments about whether the numbers will work out.

For example, suppose you are looking at properties in the $200,000 range. You already know that you will be required to make a down payment of 30 percent, and you have $60,000 set aside for that purpose. This is often as far as the analysis goes, but that can also be a mistake. You also need to study the market rent for properties like the ones you are reviewing and compare that to the mortgage payments. A lender has told you that your interest rate will probably be about 6 percent for investment property, so you also need to identify the mortgage payments you will have to make each month—in addition to allowing for property taxes, insurance, utilities, and the possibility of temporary vacancies, all as part of your cash flow analysis.

You look at a table of amortization payments, and you discover that at 6 percent, your monthly payment will be about $840 over 30 years. In addition, insurance averages about $37 per month, and property taxes run about $170. Water and disposal (utilities normally paid by the landlord) will cost an additional $32 per month. The total of *known* monthly payments will be:

Mortgage payment	$ 840
Insurance	37

Property taxes	170
Utilities	32
Total	$1,079

If you continue by comparing this *known* level of monthly obligations to market rents, you will have a fair idea of how your cash flow will work out, even before allowing for the possibility of repairs, tax or insurance increases, or vacancies. So if you discover that typical market rents for properties like this are $950 per month, there is a problem. You will be paying out more per month than you will be bringing in, even in the best of circumstances. You are going to be short by $129 per month, plus any unknown expenses.

In this situation, you need to decide on one of several courses of action:

1. *Proceed even though you know about the cash flow problem.* You may proceed in the belief that increases in property values are going to outpace the negative cash flow. This is a high-risk idea because you could be wrong or the timing of the increased market value could be further out than you expect. Furthermore, you need to be able to afford the monthly excess payout *and* any unexpected repairs. In the event of vacancies, you will need to continue paying $1,079 per month with no offsetting income, so a vacancy could be disastrous.

2. *Seek properties that cost less.* You may also look for properties in a lower price range. However, they will probably also draw less per month in market rents. When you are looking for bargain properties as an investor, you need to understand that tenants are also seeking bargains, meaning lower rents. It is likely that the relative cash flow problems will exist at each cost level.

3. *Consider multiunit buildings.* Duplex and triplex properties tend to provide better cash flow than single-family homes. While this is not always the case, it often is, and this may be worth investigating. For example, you might find that while market rents for a 2,000-square-foot single-family home average $950, a duplex with two 1,000-foot units may draw rents of $650 each, or $1,300

total—a far better scenario for approximately the same investment. You should study the differences in the market price of duplex properties and market rental rates in your area.

4. *Make a larger down payment.* You may need to invest more money to make this plan work, possibly making a considerably higher down payment. For example, at 6 percent, an $85,000 down payment would reduce the 30-year amortization to a monthly payment of about $690. Now the numbers are better:

Mortgage payment	$690
Insurance	37
Property taxes	170
Utilities	32
Total	$929

With market-rate rents at $950, this outcome is far more reasonable. However, it requires an additional $25,000 down payment; and the cash flow is still marginal.

5. *Look at properties elsewhere or wait out the market.* Realistically, the numbers may reveal that proceeding with the purchase of investment property will not work in this area, at least not yet. You may need to wait for better market-rate rentals or for a better interest rate and property price scenario.

The point of this exercise is to demonstrate that even a perfunctory examination of financial information can be very revealing. While people who invest in stocks tend to spend a lot of time analyzing fundamental and technical indicators, real estate investors often rely on advice from an agent or follow widely believed myths. These include the idea that "property values always rise" or that "negative cash flow is acceptable because market value outpaces the loss" or that "the tax benefits offset negative cash flow." There may be a degree of truth in some of these myths, but one reality worth remembering is this: You need to be able to afford the monthly cash flow. If you can't, then proceeding could be a serious mistake.

Stock market investors need to learn how to read complex financial statements and an array of confusing footnotes, and even then they may not really understand the financial condition of a company. For real estate investors, the underlying questions are usually far easier: How much money is going to come in from rents, and how much do I have to pay out?

In addition to these essential questions, the study of after-tax cash flow, return on investment, and other financial tests can be useful in comparing feasibility among properties and over time given different market conditions.

Closely related to the need to manage columns and rows of numbers and make them meaningful is the process of proration, which plays an important role in real estate. By keeping a few calculations and guidelines in mind, the rules for documenting prorations are greatly simplified. Chapter 9 explains how proration works.

PRORATED VALUES IN FINANCE AND TAXES

IMPORTANT GUIDELINES

THE NEED TO *PRORATE* real estate transactions is a constant in real estate. This need recurs in so many different aspects of the investing process that every real estate investor needs to acquire two skills: the ability to make prorations accurately *and* a rationale for making prorations that can be documented and supported.

In this chapter, you will find detailed explanations of the various forms of proration and explore methods for making a proration decision. Some of the decisions you make regarding proration may have ramifications for years to come. For example, the method you use to divide a property's value between land and improvements directly determines how much depreciation you are allowed to claim each year. There are several ways to make the proration decision, and for most people, several concerns arise when making such decisions. These include:

1. Picking the most advantageous method for making a proration

2. Documenting the rationale for the decision itself

3. Identifying alternative proration methods that may be preferable

WHY YOU NEED TO PRORATE VALUES

If you operate a business that is open to the public, you may run into proration only rarely, if ever. For example, operating a retail boutique or a consulting company involves selling goods or services, keeping track of costs and expenses, and managing a bank account. While bookkeeping for most small business operations requires skill, it is not as complex as investment accounting.

Even a generalized investing record-keeping system is often fairly straightforward. For example, stock market investors need to track different types of income sources: capital gains and losses, dividends, and interest. They may wish to compare gains and losses on an annualized basis, and they need to account for their expenses, including trading fees, sales commissions, and subscriptions.

Real estate investors face a far more complex task in keeping track of revenue and expenses. There are numerous additional, often complex record-keeping demands related to figuring out depreciation, reporting taxes, and even calculating capital gains (which may include bringing forward unclaimed losses from previous years, recapturing depreciation, and even calculating the tax basis in property when previous gains have been deferred—see Chapter 11).

Among the complexities that real estate investors face is the proration of various expenses and, in some cases, even revenue. Some examples:

1. When a tenant begins paying rent during the month, you need to prorate the first month's expenses to cover the period before the rent due date (usually the first).

2. If two or more tenants share rent, you need to calculate how much each one owes in total rent; this may involve calculations that have to include not only the space each tenant occupies, but common areas as well.

3. When you claim depreciation for items that are not specific to any one property, (for example, autos and trucks or landscaping equipment), you need to decide how to prorate that expense among the properties.

4. Operating expenses are not always specific to one property, and these also have to be prorated among properties on some basis.

5. In charging tenants for a portion of your increased property taxes, insurance, or utility costs (as may be specified in a lease

or rental contract), you need to prorate by the days affected by the increased rates. You also need to prorate among tenants in any multiunit building.

6. Property taxes are often due twice a year, but expenses apply to specific months. In some instances, the expense needs to be set up to reflect the applicable month of the expense rather than the timing of the payment. The same calculation requirement is often seen in insurance; payments may be due for 3, 6, or 12 months in advance, but it is desirable to report each month's expense in the appropriate time slot.

7. When you purchase properties, you are allowed to depreciate the improvements, but not the land. The method you use to break down your basis between these two will determine the amount of depreciation you are allowed to claim.

USEFUL PRORATION METHODS

The specific types of transactions that require proration should each be handled on the basis that makes the most sense, given the nature of the transaction. For example, in dealing with tenant-related matters, proration probably will involve prorating on the basis of a number of days or square feet of rental space. When dividing up expenses, this would most logically be done on the basis of rental income. No one method will work for every proration requirement. For this reason, you will need to study each specific area and identify the most useful method of proration.

PARTIAL MONTH RENT

One of the reasons why proration is required that anyone working with tenants will encounter most frequently arises when someone moves into or out of a rental midway through the month. This affects both the calculation of rent—either the first or the last month—and the cost of utilities. For example, if rent is due on July 1 and a tenant gives notice that she is moving out on July 12, how do you prorate rent and utilities? Some rental agreements require that notice be given through to the first of the following month, but that is inflexible, and at times people need to vacate on a date other than the end of the monthly rental period.

The applicable period for which rent is charged or credited can be calculated using one of two methods: the exact number of days or a 30-day month method. Whichever method you employ, it is wise to include the method of calculation in the rental agreement. The difference the choice of method makes depends on the month (28, 29, 30, or 31 days) involved; however, the dollar amount will not be significant. As a matter of policy, it is reasonable to suggest that you decide on a method and use it consistently.

In the actual days method, you count the number of days in the period and calculate those days as a percentage of the total month. If rent will be charged through July 12 and the month has 31 days, the formula would be to figure 12/31 of the full month's liability.

Formula: Partial Month's Rent Liability

$$\frac{D}{M} = P$$

where D = days in period to be counted
      M = full month
      P = partial month liability

The same formula applies if you use the second calculation method, assuming that all months have 30 days and the year consists of exactly 360 days. This "banker's year" is commonly used in the lending and real estate industries. In that case, the month (*M*) would always have the value 30.

The example in which a tenant gives notice through July 12 would involve dividing 12 by the full month's count. Using the 30-day-month method:

12 ÷ 30 = 0.40

If you use the alternative method, the proration in a 31-day month would be:

12 ÷ 31 = 0.39

There is little difference between these two methods. For example, based on rent of $700 per month, the difference in liability is only $7.

The procedure works on the other end of the rental period as well. For example, let's say your property is vacated on July 12 and a new tenant takes up residence on July 16. How much rent is due for the short month from July 16 through the end of the month? To apply the formula using both methods, you begin by counting the days. In a 30-day month, the period from the 16th through the 30th involves 15 days. In a 31-day month, you would use 16 days:

15 ÷ 30 = 0.50
15 ÷ 31 = 0.48

If the rent were $700 per month, the difference here is $14.00.

SHARED RENT AMONG TENANTS

A second tenant-related proration is required whenever one of two situations arises. The first is the case where two or more tenants cohabit and are responsible separately for part of the rent. The second is the case where rent applies for only part of the year, and the property is used as a second home or vacation home for the balance.

Tenants' share of property can be complex when common areas are involved. Consider this situation: You have a 2,200-square-foot house and three tenants, Bob, Josh, and Andy. Total rent is $1,100 per month. Each tenant has his own bedroom:

Bob   375 square feet
Josh   400 square feet
Andy   260 square feet

The rest of the house is shared by the three tenants, and they have agreed to pay for the entire house on a "shared" basis. But what does that mean? The solution is not as straightforward as it may seem. In some shared agreements, three tenants will simply agree to split the rent one-third each. But in this example, Andy could make a case that because his bedroom is the smallest, he should not have to pay a full one-third of the rent. Bob and Josh could argue in response that the bedroom size is not the most important aspect, but that the common areas (living room, kitchen, and so on) make the deal more equal than mere bedroom size. Some accommodation might have to be made to adjust for these arguments.

On a strictly prorated basis, the total rent would be divided using square feet. This means that Andy would pay the least amount of rent.

Formula: Prorated Rent, Tenant Share

$$\frac{T}{F} = P$$

where T = tenant's square-foot share
     F = total square feet
     P = prorated rent

In the example provided, each tenant's total rent would be calculated by first adding up the square feet of the bedrooms alone. This comes to 1,035 feet. Next, you apply the formula:

Bob	375 ÷ 1,035 =	36%
Josh	400 ÷ 1,035 =	39%
Andy	260 ÷ 1,035 =	25%
Total		100%

Applying these prorations to the total rent, $1,100, gives:

Bob	36% × $1,100 =	$ 396
Josh	39% × $1,100 =	$ 429
Andy	25% × $1,100 =	$ 275
Total	100%	$1,100

If you are to make any adjustments to these breakdowns based on emphasis on common areas and in consideration of varying bedroom sizes, the deal can be brokered using any method that makes everyone happy. If the tenants agree to round out to rents of $400/$400/$300 or to $375/$375/$350, it does not matter to you—as long as everyone is in agreement.

The multitenant situation can be quite complex. For this reason, it makes complete sense for a landlord to insist on working with one *primary tenant* who signs the agreement and is responsible for the entire rent. That tenant can then make a deal with the others according to whatever works out, allowing the landlord the simplicity of working with only one person.

PARTIAL-YEAR RENTALS

Partial-year rentals are somewhat easier to deal with than shared rent proration. In the typical partial-year rental situation, you will plan to use a property for certain months and rent it out for the rest of the year. For example, you and your family may want to use the property during the months of July and August, and for the remainder of the year it is rented out as an income property. The basis for prorating the use of the house is normally going to be the number of days the property is identified for each use, whether it is actually occupied or not. It is the *availability* that determines how much you are allowed to deduct as rental expense for tax purposes. For example, the property may be available for rent for 10 months. Even if you collect rents for only seven months, you are still allowed to claim expenses for the portion of the year the property is available.

There are three methods for calculating the proration of expenses: actual days based on the number of days in the year (365 or 366), number of days based on 30-day months and a 360-day year, and a simple division of months.

For example, suppose you rent out a property for 10 months. You are allowed to claim deductions for depreciation, interest, property taxes, insurance, utilities, and other expenses for 10/12 of the year, calculated using one of the prorated methods. For the remaining two months, you can claim interest and property taxes as itemized deductions on a second home, but other expenses cannot be deducted.

If you use the days method, the formula is based on the actual number-of-days count or on 360. For example, if your property is available for two months, the 360-day-year method would count that as 60 days. Under the actual days method, you count July and August, which both have 31 days; so that would be a total of 62 out of 365 days.

Formula: Prorated Rent, Partial-Year Use

$$\frac{R}{F} = P$$

where R = rental period
      F = full year
      P = prorated rent

Using either method produces a prorated answer:

60 ÷ 360 = 16.67%
62 ÷ 365 = 16.99%

The outcome for the two cases is very close. The decision to use the 360-day year often comes down to a matter of convenience rather than one of a significantly greater amount of deductions.

DEPRECIATION FOR NONPROPERTY ITEMS

In Chapter 11, you will find depreciation calculations in detail. For the purposes of proration, real estate investors need to decide how to handle nonspecific property depreciation. For example, you know that claiming depreciation for a building and other improvements is specific to one property. However, if you own two or more rental properties, how do you break down depreciation on a truck?

In reporting revenue and expenses for rental properties, you are required to break down deductions among properties. So the most obvious way to *assign* or *allocate* depreciation for nonproperty items is on the basis of revenue (see the next section, "Nonspecific Expense Proration"). This is logical and fairly easy to calculate, and it solves the problem. However, it also makes tracking expenses more difficult. If you prorate depreciation and other expenses, you should prepare a worksheet showing all of your calculations—not only to prepare for the possibility of a tax audit, but also so that you will know how you broke down the numbers from one year to the next. This year's worksheet makes next year's tax calculation far easier.

An alternative is to report specific expenses for each property, and then include a nonspecific expense column as well. In this column, there would be no revenue, but expenses such as depreciation, office supplies, auto and truck expenses, and professional fees are listed. This keeps reporting simple, but it may also complicate your tax reporting—especially if you are not allowed to claim a full deduction each year for reported losses. In that case, losses are carried forward and claimed against other investment income, *or* taken when properties are eventually sold. So if you have unassigned expense losses carried over, how do you assign them to individual properties when those properties are sold? Using unassigned categories works only if and when you are able to claim a deduction for your real estate losses in the current year.

NONSPECIFIC EXPENSE PRORATION

The most complex tax calculation you will need to make is that for dividing expenses among properties. Some expenses, including mortgage loan interest, property taxes, utilities, and property-specific depreciation, are easily assigned to the subject property. However, some other expenses are not specific to one property, and these have to be assigned on some basis when you own two or more rentals.

One method would be to simply divide up expenses evenly. If you own three properties, one-third of your nonspecific expenses go to each property. If you owned one property for only part of the year, it may be necessary to calculate a proportionate reduction for the year's expenses.

Formula: Expense Allocation (Even Distribution)

$$\frac{E}{P} = A$$

where E = nonspecific expenses
P = number of properties
A = allocation percentage

For example, if you own three properties, unallocated expenses would be prorated one-third to each. However, what if one of your properties was owned for only part of the year? For example, suppose you own three properties, but you acquired one of those properties at the beginning of the fourth month. This means that on the even distribution basis, the third property should be prorated a lower portion of the total.

In this case you would need to break down the proportionate level of proration for the property you owned for a shorter period. This can be done on the basis of the number of months involved. You owned properties 1 and 2 for 12 months each, and property 3 for only 8 months. The total number of months is 32 (12 + 12 + 8).

Formula: Expense Allocation (Months Owned)

$$\frac{M}{T} = A$$

where M = months of ownership during the year
      T = total months of ownership, all properties
      A = allocation percentage

Using the previous example, properties 1 and 2 would each be pro-rated 37.5 percent (12 ÷ 32), and property 3 would be prorated the remaining 25 percent of unallocated expenses (8 ÷ 32).

Another method is to break down the expenses based on a proportionate share of rental income. This is a reasonable method even when you own properties only part of the year. A shorter period would translate into lower revenues, so this formula can be used consistently no matter when properties were acquired. Under this method, you add the rental income for all properties owned during the year, then each property receives a share of prorated expenses based on its percentage of the total.

Formula: Expense Allocation (Revenue Share)

$$\frac{R}{T} = A$$

where R = revenue received for the property
      T = total revenue, all properties
      A = allocation percentage

For example, if you own three properties during the year, the first step is to add up rental revenues for all three:

Property 1	$10,800
Property 2	12,600
Property 3	7,200
Total	$30,600

Applying the formula, 35 percent of expenses would be prorated to property 1 ($10,800 ÷ $30,600), 41 percent to property 2 ($12,600 ÷ $30,600), and 24 percent to property 3 ($7,200 ÷ $30,600).

Increased Expenses Charged to Tenants

Another proration situation arises when lease or rental terms include a provision for passing on increases in certain expenses, such as property taxes, utilities, or insurance. For example, you may own a three-unit building, and each tenant has agreed to accept rent increases if and when the building's property taxes are increased. The contract's terms should define exactly how the increase is to be prorated among the three units, to avoid possible arguments in the future. Two logical methods of calculating the breakdown are on the basis of revenue (see the previous discussion) or on the basis of square feet for each unit.

Using a square-foot breakdown may be easier to support than a breakdown based on rental income. As the rent you charge may vary between units and not track square footage exactly, it may be more reliable to use square feet consistently, regardless of how much rent is charged. A tenant may rightly protest, for example, if one unit is vacant when the property tax increase comes through, and the landlord attempts to divide the expense among *two* tenants. It is not the tenant's fault that the third unit is unoccupied, and it would be more equitable to use square feet. Thus, in the event that a unit is vacant, a higher rent would apply to a new tenant.

To calculate a proration based on square feet, it makes sense to ignore gross building area and concentrate on rentable square feet only. The proration would apply to the increase in the specific expense (in this case, property tax) only, and each tenant would be required to pay a higher rent based on that allocation.

Formula: Expense Allocation (Square Feet)

$$\frac{F}{T} = A$$

where F = rentable square feet, each unit
       T = total square feet, all units
       A = allocation percentage

For example, your rental property contains three units. They measure:

Unit 1   550 square feet
Unit 2   475 square feet
Unit 3   440 square feet

Total   1,465 square feet

Applying the formula, unit 1 is responsible for 38 percent of the increase (550 ÷ 1,465), unit 2 gets 32 percent (475 ÷ 1,465), and unit 3 is prorated 30 percent.

PROPERTY TAXES AND INSURANCE CALCULATIONS

In recording transactions in your books and records, you can use several different methods. The easiest is to record expenses as they occur, even when the applicable period extends beyond the month in which payment is made. The second method involves prorating the expense over the period.

For example, you may pay an insurance premium every March and September. The March payment covers your property from April through September, and the September payment relates to the period from October until the following March. Under the *cash accounting* basis, you would simply record the insurance payment in March and in September. But if you would like to track your insurance expense from month to month, you need to prorate it. This allows you to review revenue, expenses, and profit (or loss) from one month to the next with accuracy. When you record a six-month payment in a single month, the true outcome is obscured. It may simplify your bookkeeping to use the cash basis and then make adjustments when you review monthly results, or it may be preferable to adopt a methodical system for handling prepayments for insurance, property taxes, and any other prepaid expense.

Formula: Expense Allocation (Prepayments)

$$\frac{E}{M} = A$$

where E = total prepaid expense
      M = number of months the expense relates to
      A = allocation amount

For example, your March prepayment for insurance on a rental property is $288. The period covered is six months, so each month is assigned $48, or one-sixth of the total payment ($288 ÷ 6). In this calculation, you use an amount rather than a percentage because the prepaid expense (*E*) is expressed in dollars.

LAND/BUILDING PRORATION METHODS

Investors struggle with the question of how to divide the total basis in their property investment between land and improvements. This breakdown is not provided automatically in real estate listings, and there are at least three methods for calculating the breakdown. It is necessary to make the division because the value of land cannot be depreciated. So in selecting one method over another, it is important to remember that higher improvement percentages translate into a higher depreciation deduction.

If you need and want a higher deduction, it would make sense to pick a method based on this desire. However, if you cannot deduct all of your net tax-based losses each year (see Chapter 11), a more conservative system is advisable. Because all depreciation is recaptured (eventually taxed) upon sale of the property, a lower deduction could be preferable. Choosing one method over another is a decision you should make with your tax adviser's help. Once a method is picked, it has to be used for the property consistently. It may also be wise to use the same method for all of your investment properties; in the event of an audit, using the same method for all properties supports your decision and adds credibility.

The first method is to base your allocation of total value between land and improvements on the assessed value at the time you buy a property. The depreciable portion (improvements) is expressed as a percentage of the total assessed value, and that percentage is applied against your total basis.

Formula: Depreciation Basis (Assessed Value)

$$\frac{I}{V} = A$$

where I = improvement value per assessment
     V = total assessed value
     A = allocated basis, improvements

For example, you purchase a property for $162,800. According to the assessor's office, the total assessed value of the property is $140,000, $90,000 in improvements and $50,000 for land. The depreciable basis of improvements is 64 percent ($90,000 ÷ $140,000). Applied against your total basis, this means that you can base annual depreciation on $104,200, rounded up ($162,800 × 0.64).

A second basis for depreciation is the value used by your insurance carrier. Every policy identifies what the insurer is covering. Land is excluded, since even in the case of a total loss of the building, the land would remain. The *dwelling protection* amount is expressed in terms of "limits of liability." So a partial loss would involve reimbursement for a calculated value that was not necessarily equal to the full limit. The full limit would be the basis only in the event of a total loss. This number may also serve as the basis for depreciation.

Formula: Depreciation Basis (Insured Value)

$$\frac{L}{V} = A$$

where L = insurance limits of liability, dwelling
V = total basis in the property
A = allocated basis, improvements

For example, you purchase a property, and your total basis is $162,800. Your insurance agent calculates the dwelling's limit of liability (based on age, size, and features) as $153,000. Applying the formula, your depreciable basis is 94 percent (rounded up) ($153,000 ÷ $162,800), or insured value equal to 94 percent of the price. The remaining 6 percent cannot be represented.

The third method is to base your proration on the appraiser's report. This report breaks out the value of improvements and land based on the cost approach, the sales comparison approach, or a combination of the two.

Formula: Depreciation Basis (Appraised Value)

$$\frac{I}{V} = A$$

where I = improvement value per appraisal
V = total appraised value
A = allocated basis, improvements

For example, you purchased a property, and your total basis is $162,800. The appraisal estimated the market value of the property at $165,000, and identified land value as $40,000 and improvements as $125,000. Thus, improvements are valued at 76 percent of the total market value (rounded up) ($125,000 ÷ $165,000). The basis for depreciation of improvements using this method is $123,700 (rounded down) ($162,800 × 0.76).

CONSISTENCY IN METHOD

Three final notes are worth remembering for any and all prorations you make. The first is the need to show your work and keep worksheets as part of your property records. The second is to use a method consistently, and the third is, keep it simple.

Documentation is crucial in order for you to go back in subsequent years or for subsequent properties and apply the same formulas. Your rationale for making a particular proration should be explained on the worksheet as well. For example, if you decide to break out nonspecific expenses on the basis of rental income proration, include a footnote to the calculation explaining that you consider this to be the most reliable and consistent method for allocating expenses. And if you decide to use appraised value as the basis for identifying depreciable improvements, refer back to the appraiser's report and attach a photocopy of the sheet from the appraisal showing the value of land, improvements, and the total.

Consistency is also important in the types of subjective calculations you make in your books. Because virtually every proration is an estimate, your assumptions are strengthened when you use the same method every year and for every property. If you use different methods, the decision about how you prorate expenses or identify the basis of improvements is more difficult to support or explain.

Finally, complex formulas or rationales not only are difficult to work with, but may also be difficult to explain. Avoid obscuring your rationale by picking a simple proration method whenever possible. This simplifies your record keeping as well as enabling you to make your calculations with less effort.

Chapter 10 expands upon the rules of proration to show how the principles are applied in one very important way: in the escrow and closing process. This is a process in which all transactions are documented for both buyer and seller, and invariably, you will have to split expenses or liabilities between the two sides.

CHAPTER 10

ESCROW AND CLOSING

GETTING BOTH SIDES IN BALANCE

ANYONE WHO HAS EXPERIENCED a *closing* procedure knows that it involves numerous forms and seemingly endless calculations. So many legal requirements, filings, and disclosures are involved that a closing is invariably complex and time consuming.

The U.S. Department of Housing and Urban Development (HUD) is associated with many housing programs in the real estate community. This federal agency has also developed standardized forms used in most areas for closing procedures. The *HUD-1 Settlement Statement* is used by most escrow companies, attorneys, and lenders to summarize closing transactions and to serve as a cover sheet for the large number of other forms within a closing package. A sample of this two-part form is provided in Figures 10.1a and 10.1b.

Valuable resource:

The HUD web site provides information, forms, booklets, and links for a variety of real estate–related topics. Check http://www.hud.gov.

In this chapter, you will discover how the calculations involved in closing are transferred to the form and how both buyer and seller are provided with a complete and accurate summary of the process. The various transactions involved are complex because cash goes

Figure 10.1a. HUD-1 Settlement Statement.

A. Settlement Statement U.S. Department of Housing and Urban Development   OMB Approval No. 2502-0265 (expires 9/30/2006)

B. Type of Loan

1. ☐ FHA 2. ☐ FmHA 3. ☐ Conv. Unins. 4. ☐ VA 5. ☐ Conv. Ins.	6. File Number: 7. Loan Number: 8. Mortgage Insurance Case Number:

C. Note: This form is furnished to give you a statement of actual settlement costs. Amounts paid to and by the settlement agent are shown. Items marked "(p.o.c.)" were paid outside the closing; they are shown here for informational purposes and are not included in the totals.

D. Name & Address of Borrower:	E. Name & Address of Seller:	F. Name & Address of Lender:

G. Property Location:	H. Settlement Agent:
	Place of Settlement: I. Settlement Date:

J. Summary of Borrower's Transaction		K. Summary of Seller's Transaction	
100. Gross Amount Due From Borrower		**400. Gross Amount Due To Seller**	
101. Contract sales price		401. Contract sales price	
102. Personal property		402. Personal property	
103. Settlement charges to borrower (line 1400)		403.	
104.		404.	
105.		405.	
Adjustments for items paid by seller in advance		**Adjustments for items paid by seller in advance**	
106. City/town taxes to		406. City/town taxes to	
107. County taxes to		407. County taxes to	
108. Assessments to		408. Assessments to	
109.		409.	
110.		410.	
111.		411.	
112.		412.	
120. Gross Amount Due From Borrower		**420. Gross Amount Due To Seller**	
200. Amounts Paid By Or In Behalf Of Borrower		**500. Reductions In Amount Due To Seller**	
201. Deposit or earnest money		501. Excess deposit (see instructions)	
202. Principal amount of new loan(s)		502. Settlement charges to seller (line 1400)	
203. Existing loan(s) taken subject to		503. Existing loan(s) taken subject to	
204.		504. Payoff of first mortgage loan	
205.		505. Payoff of second mortgage loan	
206.		506.	
207.		507.	
208.		508.	
209.		509.	
Adjustments for items unpaid by seller		**Adjustments for items unpaid by seller**	
210. City/town taxes to		510. City/town taxes to	
211. County taxes to		511. County taxes to	
212. Assessments to		512. Assessments to	
213.		513.	
214.		514.	
215.		515.	
216.		516.	
217.		517.	
218.		518.	
219.		519.	
220. Total Paid By/For Borrower		**520. Total Reduction Amount Due Seller**	
300. Cash At Settlement From/To Borrower		**600. Cash At Settlement To/From Seller**	
301. Gross Amount due from borrower (line 120)		601. Gross amount due to seller (line 420)	
302. Less amounts paid by/for borrower (line 220)	( )	602. Less reductions in amt. due seller (line 520)	( )
303. Cash ☐ From ☐ To Borrower		**603. Cash** ☐ To ☐ From Seller	

Section 5 of the Real Estate Settlement Procedures Act (RESPA) requires the following: • HUD must develop a Special Information Booklet to help persons borrowing money to finance the purchase of residential real estate to better understand the nature and costs of real estate settlement services; • Each lender must provide the booklet to all applicants from whom it receives or for whom it prepares a written application to borrow money to finance the purchase of residential real estate; • Lenders must prepare and distribute with the Booklet a Good Faith Estimate of the settlement costs that the borrower is likely to incur in connection with the settlement. These disclosures are manadatory.

Section 4(a) of RESPA mandates that HUD develop and prescribe this standard form to be used at the time of loan settlement to provide full disclosure of all charges imposed upon the borrower and seller. These are third party disclosures that are designed to provide the borrower with pertinent information during the settlement process in order to be a better shopper.

The Public Reporting Burden for this collection of information is estimated to average one hour per response, including the time for reviewing instructions, searching existing data sources, gathering and maintaining the data needed, and completing and reviewing the collection of information.

This agency may not collect this information, and you are not required to complete this form, unless it displays a currently valid OMB control number.

The information requested does not lend itself to confidentiality.

Figure 10.1b.

L. Settlement Charges			Paid From Borrowers Funds at Settlement	Paid From Seller's Funds at Settlement
700. Total Sales/Broker's Commission based on price $		@　% =		
Division of Commission (line 700) as follows:				
701. $	to			
702. $	to			
703. Commission paid at Settlement				
704.				
800. Items Payable In Connection With Loan				
801. Loan Origination Fee	%			
802. Loan Discount	%			
803. Appraisal Fee	to			
804. Credit Report	to			
805. Lender's Inspection Fee				
806. Mortgage Insurance Application Fee to				
807. Assumption Fee				
808.				
809.				
810.				
811.				
900. Items Required By Lender To Be Paid In Advance				
901. Interest from　to	@ $	/day		
902. Mortgage Insurance Premium for		months to		
903. Hazard Insurance Premium for		years to		
904.		years to		
905.				
1000. Reserves Deposited With Lender				
1001. Hazard insurance	months @ $	per month		
1002. Mortgage insurance	months @ $	per month		
1003. City property taxes	months @ $	per month		
1004. County property taxes	months @ $	per month		
1005. Annual assessments	months @ $	per month		
1006.	months @ $	per month		
1007.	months @ $	per month		
1008.	months @ $	per month		
1100. Title Charges				
1101. Settlement or closing fee	to			
1102. Abstract or title search	to			
1103. Title examination	to			
1104. Title insurance binder	to			
1105. Document preparation	to			
1106. Notary fees	to			
1107. Attorney's fees	to			
(includes above items numbers:		)		
1108. Title insurance	to			
(includes above items numbers:		)		
1109. Lender's coverage	$			
1110. Owner's coverage	$			
1111.				
1112.				
1113.				
1200. Government Recording and Transfer Charges				
1201. Recording fees: Deed $	; Mortgage $	; Releases $		
1202. City/county tax/stamps: Deed $	; Mortgage $			
1203. State tax/stamps: Deed $	; Mortgage $			
1204.				
1205.				
1300. Additional Settlement Charges				
1301. Survey　to				
1302. Pest inspection to				
1303.				
1304.				
1305.				
1400. Total Settlement Charges (enter on lines 103, Section J and 502, Section K)				

to and from several different people: the buyer, the seller, the escrow agent or attorney, and the lender. A methodical process of accounting for these transactions makes the process easier to understand.

The most complex calculations involve prorations because these may be calculated under several different systems. So the initial mathematical problems will be best understood by understanding how proration works during the closing process.

The complexity of figuring out the basis in property for tax purposes may also be complex. Both buyer and seller have to adjust the price of the property for closing costs (buyers add these costs to find the adjusted purchase price, and sellers subtract these costs from their price to find the adjusted sales price). The calculation becomes even more complex in defining the basis in property. Tax rules allow investors to defer capital gains if a precise procedure is followed. However, the amount of deferred gain reduces the basis in the replacement property. So closing math involves several calculations, but the documentation is essential for ensuring that calculations of basis and tax liability are based on well-established, actual numbers.

REAL ESTATE CLOSING PRORATIONS

The math involved in closings is not limited to documenting an agreed-upon price, moving funds between lenders and sellers, or paying for title insurance. It invariably involves the need to make several prorations.

It is rare for a closing to occur on a date where no prorations would be required. A number of different prorations are likely to be included in the closing calculations for mortgage interest, property taxes, rent (when tenants are involved or when a buyer or seller does not exchange property on the day of closing), and utilities. Prorations can be made using several different methods. For example, whole or fractional months or weeks can be used to divide up some types of obligations, the 30-day month and 360-day year are easily calculated, or the exact number of days can be used. In all of the examples that follow, the exact number of days is used.

The following discussion expands on Chapter 9's description

of proration as it applies specifically to escrow situations. Calculating the exact number of days, for example, is used for figuring out mortgage interest, property taxes, and utilities.

MORTGAGE INTEREST

Mortgage interest prorations are needed to figure out the interest due on a loan right up to the day of closing. Interest is charged in advance, so the lender who has approved a buyer's loan is entitled to collect interest from the date of closing to the first payment due date. For example, suppose your escrow closes on March 18, and your first mortgage payment will be due on April 1. The loan was granted at 6.0 percent with a 30-year amortization. Your loan amount is $87,000. The number of days from closing on March 18 through the end of the month is 13 days. To calculate 13 days' interest, you need to (1) compute the annual interest, (2) divide by 12 to arrive at the monthly interest, and (3) figure interest for 13 days.

Formula: Closing Prorated Interest

$$\frac{L \times I}{12} \times \frac{D}{M} = P$$

where L = loan amount
       I = interest rate
       D = days of prorated interest
       M = days in the month
       P = prorated interest

In this example, the loan amount is $87,000 and annual interest is 6.0 percent (decimal equivalent 0.06), and you need to figure out 13 days' interest in March, which has 31 days. Applying the formula:

[($87,000 × 0.06) ÷ 12] × (13 ÷ 31) = $182.42

PROPERTY TAXES

In most communities, property taxes are due in semiannual installments. For example, the total property tax bill is divided into two parts, covering the periods from January 1 through June 30 and from July 1 through December 31. Payments are due on April 30 and October 31 each year. In this situation, a March 18 closing will require a proration. If the seller has not paid the first half of the installment due April 30, then the seller's responsibility is for the days up to the closing.

Formula: Closing Prorated Property Taxes

$$T \times \frac{D}{L} = P$$

where T = total property tax bill, half-year
      D = days of responsibility
      L = days in liability period
      P = prorated property taxes

For example, if the half-year liability for property taxes is $1,153.16, how much is the seller responsible for on March 18? There are 77 days in the period (31 in January, 28 in February, and 18 in March), and the liability period of January 1 through June 30 contains 181 days (31 + 28 + 31 + 30 + 31 + 30). Applying the formula:

$1,153.16 \times (77 \div 181) = \$490.57$

The seller is responsible for $490.57, the prorated liability for the 77 days. This may work in reverse as well. Consider the situation where closing occurs on May 12, for example. In this case, you may assume that the seller has already paid the half-year liability, covering the period from January 1 through June 30. But with the closing occurring on May 12, the buyer is responsible for 49 days' liability, from May 12 through June 30 (19 days + 30 days). In this case, the *buyer* would be responsible for a prorated portion of taxes:

$1,153.16 \times (49 \div 181) = \$312.18$

Prorations also are used when either the buyer or the seller possesses the property before or after closing. In those cases, the same procedure is used, with rental income and expense used in place of property tax liabilities. Additionally, when utilities are partially assigned to buyer and seller, the same formula is used, with the total utility bill used as the basis for division using number of days.

Various methods can also be used to break out the number of days. For example, you can base the calculation on 30-day months and a 360-day year. It is more likely that these kinds of prorated responsibilities will be based on the exact number of days involved. Calculating the number of days in an applicable period for prorating is based on the number of days in each month. Table 10.1 provides a useful summary.

This table makes it easy and fast to calculate the number of days to be prorated, whether they are charged to the buyer or the seller. By adding the applicable number of days to the count in the last completed month, you can easily calculate the proration period. For example, to find the number of days applicable to the seller as of March 18, add the 18 days to the day count as of the end of February (18 + 59 = 77). To find the number of days applicable to the buyer, you can either subtract the result of this calculation from the total number of days in the year (365 − 77 = 288) or subtract the seller's 18 days from the remaining number of days in the previous month (306 − 18 = 288).

Table 10.1.   Proration Table: Number of Days.*

Month	Days	Days in the Year Used	Remaining
January	31	31	334
February	28*	59	306
March	31	90	275
April	30	120	245
May	31	151	214
June	30	181	184
July	31	212	153
August	31	243	122
September	30	273	92
October	31	304	61
November	30	334	31
December	31	365	0

*In leap years, the total days in the year must be increased to 366 days and February must be increased to 29 days.

Formula: Closing Prorated Days (Seller)

$U + D = P$

where U = days used as of prior month-end
      D = days in partial month
      P = prorated days, seller

Formula: Closing Prorated Days (Buyer)

$R - D = P$

where R = days remaining as of prior month-end
      D = days in partial month
      P = prorated days, buyer

THE SETTLEMENT STATEMENT

The prorated obligations may go in either direction. The seller may owe a portion of a liability to the buyer, or vice versa. Some prorations are assigned to one side only. For example, mortgage interest for a partial month is a buyer's obligation; it does not affect the seller.

A large volume of transactions have to be accounted for on the closing statement, including not only prorations but the exchange of funds among buyer, seller, escrow agent, and lender. The settlement statement is a two-column report showing two sides. On the left is the itemized detail adding up to the total gross amount due from the borrower. On the right is the total gross amount due to the seller.

The buyer's side includes the initial sales price plus any personal property included in the deal, plus settlement charges (buyer's closing costs). Adjustments (these are where prorations are itemized) can be added to or subtracted from this itemized list. Payments made by the borrower reduce the gross amount due and include an earnest money deposit and the principal of the loan (provided by the lender). The net difference is the amount the borrower owes at closing. This consists of the down payment (unless it has already been placed on deposit in escrow) plus and minus all of the adjustments.

The seller's side begins with the same contract sales price plus the value of personal property being exchanged. Prorated obligations are added to or subtracted from this total. Additional reductions include settlement charges (seller's closing costs), payoff of all existing mortgage loans, and any sales commissions payable to a real estate agent. The net difference between the sales amount and the remaining adjustments is the amount to be paid to the seller upon closing.

The buyer, the seller, and the real estate broker are all parties to the closing, and every entry added to one of the three is subtracted elsewhere or, when no offsetting payment or credit is involved, changes the balance at the bottom of the statement. Here is an extended example:

You purchased a rental property for $130,000. You made a $43,000 down payment offer based on an earnest money deposit of $3,000, contingent on approval of financing for $87,000. Buyer's settlement charges were $1,160.50. You closed on March 18, and you also had the following prorations: As buyer, you were obligated for mortgage interest of $182.42 and utilities of $44.32. The seller was prorated $490.57 in property taxes for the portion of the year between January 1 and March 18.

In addition, there was a payoff of the seller's existing loan in the amount of $47,351 and a real estate commission of $7,800. As buyer, you also had to pay for one year's insurance of $411, title insurance premium and title search totaling $644, and $2,454 in other closing costs.

Based on these figures, the settlement statement would appear like the sample in Table 10.2.

ADJUSTED PURCHASE AND SALE PRICE, AND BASIS IN PROPERTY

In calculating the amount of proceeds to go to the seller and to come from the buyer, the series of transactions is listed and documented with various attachments. The next step for both sides is a calculation of the *basis* in the property being bought or sold.

Basis means something beyond price. The price a buyer pays for property is only the starting point in calculating basis. Because a capital gain is calculated with basis as a starting point, you also need to know how the adjusted basis in property is derived, how it

Table 10.2.   Settlement Statement.

Summary of Borrower's Transactions		Summary of Seller's Transactions	
Gross amount due from borrower:		**Gross amount due to seller:**	
Contract sales price	$130,000.00	Contract sales price	$130,000.00
Settlement charges to			
borrower	1,160.50		
Mortgage interest	182.42		
Adjustments for items paid by seller in advance:		*Adjustments for items paid by seller in advance:*	
Utilities	44.32	Utilities	44.32
Insurance, one year	411.00		
Title insurance costs	644.00		
Gross amount due from		Gross amount due to	
borrower	132,442.24	seller	130,044.32
Amounts paid by or in behalf of borrower:		**Reductions in amount due to seller:**	
Deposit or earnest money	3,000.00		
Principal amount of new			
loan(s)	87,000.00	Settlement charges to seller 7,800.00	
		Payoff of first mortgage lien 47,351.00	
Adjustments for items unpaid by seller:		*Adjustments for items unpaid by seller:*	
Property taxes	490.57	Property taxes	490.57
Total paid by or for		Total reduction in amount	
borrower	90,490.57	due seller	55,641.57
Cash at settlement from/to borrower		**Cash at settlement to/from seller**	
Gross amount due from		Gross amount due to	
borrower	132,442.24	seller	130,044.32
Less amounts paid by/for		Less reductions in amount	
borrower	90,490.57	due to seller	55,641.57
Cash from borrower	41,951.67	Cash to seller	74,402.75

is adjusted over a holding period, and how the basis in new property may be affected by the way an old property is sold.

In Chapter 11, an exploration of income taxes relating to real estate investing includes many topics related to the question of basis. For now, you will be concerned primarily with the way in which adjusted purchase price and adjusted sales price are calculated and how basis is developed. The first step is figuring the *adjusted purchase price* of property. This is the price paid plus closing costs. It is not the same as the adjusted *basis* in property, which includes purchase price, closing costs, and any deferred gains from a previous sale of property. The adjusted purchase price is used in more basic situations, where no deferred gain from another property is involved.

Formula: Adjusted Purchase Price

P + C = A

where P = purchase price
       C = closing costs
       A = adjusted purchase price

For example, in the exercise, the purchase price was $130,000 and the buyer had to pay additional settlement costs of $1,160.50. For investment property, the prorated items and additional expenses would normally be treated as first-year expenses, to be deducted from rental income. This includes interest for the partial month, utilities, and insurance. The adjusted purchase price in this example would be:

$130,000.00 + $1,160.50 = $131,160.50

The adjusted sales price is calculated in a similar manner; however, instead of closing costs being added to the price, they are subtracted, meaning that those costs reduce the cash the seller receives.

Formula: Adjusted Sales Price

S − C = A

where S = sales price
       C = closing costs
       A = adjusted sales price

In this example, the sales price is $130,000.00 and the seller's closing costs are $7,800.00. So the adjusted sales price would be:

$130,000.00 − $7,800.00 = $122,200.00

The buyer may have additional calculations to perform. If this property is the buyer's first investment property, the adjusted purchase price also becomes the *basis* in the property. However, as explained in more detail in Chapter 11, investors are allowed to defer capital gains on real estate investments through a *like-kind exchange*, also called a 1031 exchange (named after the code section in which this provision is explained). If investors meet the rules, they can defer paying taxes on a capital gain as long as they replace one property with another.

For example, if you assume that the investor had sold a previous property and purchased the new one, any gains would be deferred. At the same time, the basis in the new property would be reduced by the amount of deferred gain. For example, let's assume that you had bought a property, held it for five years, and reported the following profit:

Sales price	$119,500
Less closing costs	9,443
Adjusted sales price	$110,057
Original purchase price	$ 82,000
Plus closing costs	915
Adjusted purchase price	$ 82,915
Minus depreciation	9,091
Adjusted basis	$ 73,824
Capital gain	$ 36,233

In this example, the capital gain is computed by calculating the difference between the adjusted sales price and the original basis. However, since this is an investment property, you are allowed to claim depreciation for improvements. At the time the property is sold, the basis is reduced by the amount of depreciation in the property. Now let's say you sold this property through a deferred exchange. In that case, your basis in the new property would be reduced by the amount of the gain.

Formula: Adjusted Basis in Property

$(P + C = A) - D = B$

where P = purchase price
      C = closing costs
      A = adjusted purchase price
      D = deferred gain
      B = basis in property

In the example, this formula would involve calculating the adjusted purchase price for the new property, then reducing that basis by the amount of deferred gain on the previous investment:

($130,000.00 + $1,160.50) − $36,233 = $94,927.50

This answer—the adjusted basis in the property—will be used as the starting point in calculating the capital gain when the current property is sold. So instead of starting out with an adjusted purchase price of $131,160.50, you would begin with an adjusted basis of $94,927.50. Thus, you would pay capital gains tax on the higher profit resulting from the deferral.

Chapter 11 explains how capital gains apply in real estate investments, as well as related tax rules. Real estate investors are allowed to deduct expenses and report net losses, which is a special provision not available to other investors. In tracking cash flow, the tax benefits may actually create a feasible situation in cases where, without those benefits, investors would experience negative cash flow.

CHAPTER 11

TAX CALCULATIONS IN REAL ESTATE

REPORTING RULES

REAL ESTATE HAS THE MOST COMPLEX tax rules of all investment markets. The income tax rules generally do *not* allow investors to deduct losses on real estate programs, unless those losses offset similar gains or, when properties are sold, reduce the net gain that is reported. So those who place money in limited partnerships today—which were favored tax shelter programs many years ago—cannot use those programs to produce losses.

When it comes to direct ownership of rental property, the rules are different. Real estate investors are allowed to deduct annual losses. This makes real estate the last remaining legal tax shelter, a feature that draws many people to this market. The difference that tax savings can make in the overall cash flow often justifies an investment that would otherwise not produce a positive or breakeven outcome. For many, the difference consists of the reduction in personal taxes.

REPORTING RENTAL INCOME AND LOSS

The first rule to be aware of in getting a grasp of real estate tax rules is the limitation on deductions for *passive losses*. By definition, passive income is any income from activities that you do not manage directly. So a limited partnership, in which general partners make all of the decisions and limited partners have no say in management, is a form of passive activity.

In the tax shelter days, limited partners could deduct losses without limitation. Because depreciation rules were liberal, it was possible for higher-income-bracket investors to claim deductions far above the amount they invested. For example, in some programs, it was possible for someone to invest $10,000 and claim a loss of $30,000. Because the loss was three times greater than the amount invested, such a program was referred to as a "3-to-1" write-off. Up until the early 1980s, the top tax bracket was 50 percent, so claiming a deduction for a $30,000 "loss" produced tax savings of $15,000:

Net loss	$30,000
Tax rate, 50%	−15,000
Tax savings	$15,000
Less amount invested	−10,000
Net savings	$ 5,000

The abuse of the system was so widespread that new tax laws were enacted. Among the most important was the Tax Reform Act of 1986 (TRA). This law and other reforms meant to curtail tax shelter programs included three important changes in the tax rules:

1. *Passive loss restrictions.* Losses from investments were no longer allowed when investors did not "materially participate" in the management of the property. Such losses had to be offset against passive gains or carried forward until the properties were sold.

2. *At-risk rules.* Under the old rules, investors could claim losses far higher than their actual investment basis. One scheme involved purchasing art at one amount, then getting a high appraisal and donating the art to a museum. This created a big loss. For example, buying art for $10,000 and donating it at an appraised value of $50,000 created a huge tax write-off. The new *at-risk* rules limited deductions to the amount actually put

into a program through cash or notes that had to be paid at some time in the future.

3. *Revised depreciation rules.* Under the old tax system, real estate could be depreciated rapidly using accelerated methods. For example, an investor could claim depreciation losses over a relatively short number of years and at accelerated rates. Under today's rules, residential property has to be depreciated, without acceleration, over 27.5 years.

The material participation rule distinguishes directly owned real estate from a passive investment. In a limited partnership, for example, the limited participants are by definition not materially involved in managing the investments. But when you select properties, interview tenants, collect rent, perform or supervise repairs, and make other important decisions on your own, you probably meet the standard for material participation. The law says that *material* means regular, continuous, and substantial. That means that landlords need to set rent levels, approve major expenses, and qualify tenants. Even if the day-to-day decisions are made by a management company, you can still qualify under the material participation rule. The qualification is important because in order to deduct losses, you need to meet this standard.

The maximum loss you can claim each year is $25,000. You can deduct up to this amount as long as you materially participate and as long as your adjusted gross income is below $100,000. If your income is above that level, your maximum allowable deduction for real estate losses is reduced by 50 cents for each dollar of excess.

Formula: Maximum Loss Allowance

$$\$25,000 - \frac{A - \$100,000}{2} = L$$

where A = adjusted gross income
L = maximum loss allowed

For example, if your adjusted gross income is below $100,000, all of your net losses up to $25,000 can be deducted. But if your gross income is higher, an adjustment has to be made. If your adjusted gross is $106,000, for example, the maximum allowed loss would be:

$$\$25,000 - [(\$106,000 - \$100,000) \div 2] = \$22,000$$

An additional adjustment also has to be made. Under normal circumstances, "adjusted gross income" refers to gross income for tax purposes, minus adjustments to gross income (for IRA contributions, student loan interest, moving expenses, and other such items). However, for this calculation, you need to use what is called *modified adjusted gross income*. This is normally gross income without adjustments. You cannot deduct student loan interest, IRA contributions, self-employment tax deductions, or tuition, for example. So if your adjustments to gross income are substantial, it could raise the modified AGI, changing the calculation of maximum deductible real estate losses.

PRORATED EXPENSES

The tax rules are beneficial for directly managed real estate, even with the complexities of computing allowable deductions and calculating depreciation (explained in the "Depreciation Methods" section later in this chapter). The method of reporting rental income and expenses is further complicated by a requirement that each property has to be itemized separately. Schedule E is the tax form used for summarizing real estate profit or loss. Each property has to be listed in a separate column. This becomes important if and when you cannot deduct the entire loss you report each year; those losses may need to be carried over and claimed as a reduction of profit upon sale of the property. So when you have several properties, you also need a record of how expenses were broken down among them.

There are two important proration tasks, given the quirky tax rules. The first is how you assign expenses to each property when those expenses do not specifically pertain to any one property. The second is how to track and assign excess net losses. In both instances, the most consistent and reasonable method is based on a proration of rental income. You previously saw how expenses are prorated based on the percentage of the rent earned by each property. To review: You own three properties. The total rents received last year were:

Property A	$11,450	34.3%
Property B	9,447	28.3
Property C	12,500	37.4
Total	$33,397	100.0%

This proration, which is called "expense allocation, revenue share," is used to assign expenses such as depreciation on a truck or landscaping equipment, professional fees, and telephone expense. The specific expenses that you can identify as pertaining to individual properties (such as mortgage interest, property taxes, insurance, and utilities) are simply assigned to the column for each property individually.

The second area in which proration is required involves assigning carryover losses for future deduction. It would not be reasonable to claim all carryover losses against the first property sold, because some form of orderly proration is more reasonable. So you can break down and track losses based on the proration of net losses.

Formula: Carryover Loss Allocation

$$\frac{L}{T} = A$$

where L = loss reported for the property
       T = total net loss, all properties
       A = allocation percentage

For example, if you owned three properties, you may have the following losses reported for the year:

Property A	$ 3,200
Property B	7,150
Property C	8,114
Total	$18,464

If your modified adjusted gross income for the year was $126,000, your maximum deductible loss is reduced from $25,000 to $12,000 ($25,000 less one-half the gross above $100,000, or $13,000 = $12,000 net). This provides you with an excess of $6,464 for the year ($18,464 less the maximum of $12,000). This loss can be assigned on the basis of prorated overall net losses:

Property A	$ 3,200	17.3% × $6,464 =	$1,118
Property B	7,150	38.7 × $6,464 =	$2,502
Property C	8,114	44.0 × $6,464 =	$2,844
Total	$18,464	100.0%	$6,464

A complication arises when some properties have net losses, but others have gains. In these situations, you should calculate the proration of carryover loss using *only* the properties with reported net losses; leave properties on which a gain is reported out of the equation. This occurs when depreciation for one property is lower than average, or when one property's mortgage interest is below the average. For example, let's assume that the reported outcome for the three properties included the following breakdown:

Property A	$(3,200) loss
Property B	(7,150) loss
Property C	8,119 profit
Net	$(2,231) loss

Let's also assume that your modified adjusted gross income was $148,000. In this situation, your maximum deduction would be reduced by $24,000 (one-half the income above $100,000), so your allowable net loss will be only $1,000. The carryover should be assigned to the two properties reporting a net loss on a prorated basis. The other property is excluded because it reported a gain. So the excess carryover loss will be $1,231 ($2,231 minus $1,000):

Property A	$ (3,200) loss	30.9% × $1,231 =	$ 380
Property B	(7,150) loss	69.1 × $1,231 =	$ 851
Net	$(10,350) loss	100.0%	$1,231

▨ Reporting the Sale of Property

Year-to-year gains or losses on investment property are reported on Schedule E. Capital gains are reported on Form 4797 and Schedule D. The reporting procedure requires calculation of the net capital gain or loss. A capital loss deduction is limited to a maximum of $3,000 per year, so any losses above that level have to be carried forward and applied in future years.

Our concern here is with how the net capital gain or loss is computed. While a simple example of a capital gain can be defined as the difference between the purchase price and the sale price, the calculation for real estate involves four additional calculations:

1. *Adjusted purchase price including any deferred gains.* The actual purchase price of the property may not be identical to its basis. For example, if the property was purchased through a deferred gain, the gain is brought forward and used to reduce the basis in the new property.

2. *Adjustments for unclaimed carryover losses.* Any losses that were not used and have been carried forward are added to the basis in the property (or deducted from the realized sale price), which has the effect of reducing the reported capital gain.

3. *Recapture of depreciation.* All depreciation claimed during the time the property was owned is deducted from the basis (or added to the sale price), so the gain is increased and more taxes are due (or a net loss is reduced).

4. *Calculation of adjusted sale price.* The adjusted sale price is the agreed-upon price minus closing costs.

Formula: Capital Gain or Loss

$(S - C) - L + D - (P - C - G) = N$

where S = sale price
         C = closing costs
         L = carryover losses
         D = depreciation claimed
         P = purchase price
         G = deferred gains
         N = net capital gain or loss

For example, assume the following: The property you sold this year went for $162,500, minus closing costs of $10,260. You also had carryover losses of $9,315. Depreciation claimed during the property's holding period was $18,440. The original purchase price was $120,000 less closing costs of $2,100. However, the purchase was made as part of a tax-deferred exchange involving a gain on a previous sale of $14,200. The net capital gain will be:

Sale price		$162,500
Less closing costs		− 10,260
Adjusted sales price		$152,240
Carryover losses		− 9,315
Depreciation		18,440
Original purchase price	$120,000	
Less closing costs	− 2,100	
Less deferred gain	− 14,200	
Net basis		− 103,700
Net capital gain		$ 57,665

The overall effect of this is to report a net gain that accounts for the actual profit, adjusted for depreciation and carryover losses, and to calculate the taxes due based on the net gain. In the case of a net loss, the maximum of $3,000 per year applies, and any excess has to be carried forward and used in future years.

DEPRECIATION METHODS

Many of the real estate calculations used to arrive at after-tax cash flow and capital gains involve *depreciation* expense. This expense does not involve payments of cash, but is a calculated annual allowance. You are allowed to claim depreciation based on the type of property and its depreciable basis. In the case of real estate, land cannot be depreciated, and improvements have to be written off (depreciated) over a period of 27.5 years using the *straight-line* method (meaning that the same amount is claimed each year). Other types of property (vehicles or landscaping equipment, for example) can be depreciated over shorter periods and on an accelerated basis. This means that a higher deduction is allowed in the earlier years, and the deduction declines over the course of the recovery period. Straight-line depreciation is the easiest to calculate.

Formula: Straight-Line Depreciation

$$\frac{B}{P} = D$$

where B = basis of asset
    P = period (in years)
    D = annual depreciation

Some assets can be depreciated using *accelerated depreciation* methods. Under the most common method, the annual allowance for accelerated depreciation is based on the straight-line method, but with higher depreciation allowed in the earlier years.

Formula: Accelerated Depreciation

$$\frac{B}{P} \times R = D$$

where B = basis of asset
    P = period (in years)
    R = acceleration rate
    D = annual depreciation

For example, if the acceleration rate is 150 percent, each year's depreciation would be 150 percent higher than straight-line depreciation, based on the undepreciated basis of the asset at the beginning of the year. If the asset is valued at $7,000 and you are depreciating the asset over seven years, the straight-line rate would be $1,000 per year for each of the seven years. In accelerated depreciation, however, each year's depreciation would be:

Year	Depreciation Basis	Straight-Line	Acceleration Rate	Depreciation
1	$7,000	$1,000	150%	$1,500
2	5,500	786	150%	1,179
3	4,321	617	150%	926
4	3,395	485	150%	728
5	2,667	381	150%	572

| 6 | 2,095 | 299 | 150% | 449 |
| 7 | 1,646 | 235 | 150% | 353 |

In practice, use of the accelerated method involves reverting to straight-line in the last few years. The IRS has published tables showing how to compute depreciation under each method and what percentages to claim as depreciation each year.

Valuable resource:

To order Form 4562 (used to report depreciation) or the publication providing instructions and tables for each depreciation method, check the IRS web site at http://www.irs.ustreas.gov.

Two so-called *conventions* are also used to simplify the calculation for the first year. You are not allowed to claim a full year's depreciation expense for the year in which an asset is first placed into service. Depending on the type of asset, you are required to use either the half-year convention or the mid-month convention.

The half-year convention makes all calculations within a class of assets uniform each year. The first-year calculation is based on the assumption that newly acquired assets were purchased exactly halfway through the year.

Formula: Half-Year Convention

$$\frac{B}{2} = H$$

where B = basis of the asset
       H = half-year depreciation base, first-year

For example, suppose the basis of an asset is $80,000. Using the half-year convention, first-year depreciation will be based on the assumption that the asset was acquired one-half of the way through the year:

$80,000 \div 2 = $40,000$

This does not change the basis of the asset; the full basis of $80,000 is used in subsequent years. An alternative method for figuring this out would be to first calculate depreciation, and then reduce the amount by half.

In the mid-month convention, the first-year rate is computed on the assumption that all assets in a particular class were put into service exactly halfway through the acquisition month. Thus, if you acquire an asset in January, under the mid-month convention, the depreciation would be calculated as though the asset were in service for $11\frac{1}{2}$ months of the year.

Formula: Mid-Month Convention

$$\left(\frac{B}{24}\right) \times P = M$$

where B = basis of the asset
       P = number of half-month periods
       M = mid-month depreciation basis, first year

For example, if the basis of an asset was $80,000 and it was acquired at any time during January, the first step would be to divide the basis by 24 (half-month periods), and then to multiply the sum by the number of periods the asset was in service. From January 16 through December 31, there are 23 half-month periods. Applying the formula:

($80,000 ÷ 24) × 23 = $76,667

Rounded up, depreciation for the first year would be based on this reduced basis. If the asset had been acquired in May, there would remain 15 half-month periods, so the calculation would then be:

($80,000 ÷ 24) × 15 = $50,000

An alternative is to first calculate depreciation and then apply the applicable number of periods. For example, if the straight-line method were to apply and the period was 27.5 years, first-year depreciation for an asset acquired in May would be:

($80,000 ÷ 27.5 years) × (15 ÷ 24) = $1,818

You can verify this calculation by returning to the previous method, where you concluded that the first-year basis for depreciation was $50,000. Again applying the assumption of straight-line rate and 27.5 years,

$50,000 ÷ 27.5 years = $1,818

Both methods produce the same result. In this case, subsequent-year depreciation would be based on the original $80,000 basis and 27.5 years in the recovery period:

$80,000 ÷ 27.5 years = $2,909

You would be allowed to claim a depreciation deduction over 27.5 years in the amount of $2,909 per year (after the first year). Each year's depreciation will be:

Year 1	$ 1,818
Years 2–27 ($2,909 × 26)	75,634
Year 28 (remaining balance)	2,548
Total depreciation	$80,000

The rules for depreciation are not complex, given that the IRS publishes a series of tables providing guidance as to how each class of assets is to be depreciated each year. A wise move is to calculate depreciation once for the entire recovery period and then write in each year's amount on a worksheet.

GAIN DEFERRAL FOR INVESTMENT PROPERTY

The final point concerning taxes on real estate brings us to yet another significant tax benefit: As a real estate investor, you can put off paying taxes on your capital gains. A stock market investor who sells stock at a profit pays taxes in the year in which the sale is completed and cannot simply replace the stock with the stock of another company. As a real estate investor, however, you enjoy considerable tax advantages.

Even homeowners have the extraordinary benefit of being allowed to deduct up to $500,000 of capital gains on the profit from selling their *primary residence*. (This applies to married couples; single filers and heads of household can deduct up to $250,000.) By definition, your primary residence is the home that you have lived in for at least 24 months out of the last 60 months. Conceivably, you could have two primary residences within a five-year period. However, you can claim a tax-free profit from such a sale only once every 24 months at the most. Beyond that, there are no restrictions. So a married couple could claim a tax-free sale as often as every two years.

This raises some interesting possibilities for real estate investors. You can rent out a property for many years, claim depreciation and other expenses, and then convert that property to your primary residence. As long as you live there for at least 24 months, you do not have to pay taxes on the capital gain, with one exception: You do have to declare as income the amount of depreciation claimed during the period when the property was used as investment property, and pay taxes on that amount.

Another attractive feature is the *1031 exchange* (also called a like-kind exchange), which provides that you are allowed to defer the gain on property as long as you meet specific rules. These include the requirement that you find a replacement property and close its sale within six months after you place the previous property on the market. You also need to purchase properties that cost as much as the sale price of the previous property. (If you do not exceed that price, the difference is taxed in the year of sale, and only the remaining profit can be deferred.)

Valuable resource:

The IRS publishes a useful article explaining the rules for the 1031 exchange. It can be viewed at the IRS web site, located at http://www.irs .gov/businesses/small/industries/article/0,,id = 98491,00.html. The National Association of Realtors also publishes extensive tutorials, forms, and links on the same subject at http://www.irs.gov/businesses/small/ industries/article/0,,id = 98491,00.html.

When you replace one property with another and use the 1031 exchange, the deferred gain is carried forward and used to reduce the basis in the new property. In theory, you could continue to defer profits on investment property over a period of many years. A simplified example is shown in Table 11.1.

In this example, the amount of deferred gain increases with each subsequent purchase and replacement. As long as you replace a sold house with another of equal or greater value, and as long as the transaction is completed within 180 days, you are allowed to use the 1031 exchange to defer paying taxes on investment real estate.

This is not the same as avoiding taxes altogether. The liability eventually has to be paid. However, this beneficial rule allows you to put off making the tax payment until some time in the future. In a 1031 exchange, computation of the new basis requires adjusting for the accumulated deferred gain from previous sales.

Formula: New Basis in 1031 Exchange

P − D = N

where P = adjusted purchase price
       D = deferred gain
       N = new basis

You saw an example of this process in Table 11.1. For property D, the purchase price was $142,000, but that basis was reduced by $57,000 in deferred gains on previous property transactions. Thus, upon the sale on that property, the investor reports a profit of $80,000 (the current gain of $23,000 plus accumulated deferred gains of $20,000 on property B and $37,000 on property C)—or,

Table 11.1.   Like-Kind Exchange.

Description	Property A	Property B	Property C	Property D
Adjusted sale price	$85,000	$105,000	$130,000	$165,000
Adjusted purchase price	$65,000	$ 88,000	$110,000	142,000
Less: deferred gain	0	20,000	37,000	57,000
Adjusted basis	$65,000	$ 68,000	$ 73,000	$ 85,000
Profit	$20,000	$ 37,000	$ 57,000	$ 80,000

if this is practical, the investor can continue deferring the gain by using the 1031 exchange again.

The 1031 exchange is allowed for real estate investors, but not for any others. This feature adds to the attractiveness of real estate. Additionally, you decide when to sell property or when to continue holding it. You can time either a 1031 exchange (based on market conditions, for example) or a taxable final sale (based on your current-year income and financial situation). The 1031 exchange is a superb feature in the tax law, enabling investors to continually trade up and accumulate wealth while improving their cash flow—all without having a portion of their equity taken in the form of income taxes.

When you consider the combined features of the tax-deferred exchange and the yearly tax benefits (such as being allowed to claim losses from real estate activity), the potential risks associated with cash flow and market forces often are worth taking. Dealing with tenants, lenders, and real estate agents can be complex, and for some people, this excludes real estate as a viable investment. For those investors, hiring a professional management company often solves the problem. For other investors, who enjoy working with tenants and the other people involved, real estate investing is complex and challenging, but it can also be exceptionally rewarding—as a tax shelter, a generator of positive cash flow, and a profitable long-term investment.

The next—and final—chapter, Chapter 12, shows how various building and land measurements are calculated. These are essential for anyone who is interested in raw land purchases, or for figuring out exactly how to compare two or more potential investments on the basis of actual square feet.

LAND, LOT, AND BUILDING MEASUREMENTS

CALCULATING DOWN TO THE FOOT

REAL ESTATE INVESTORS NEED TO EMPLOY many different skills in managing their properties. Included in these are land and building measurements. The geometry involved in figuring out land size or internal square feet does not have to be complicated; if you follow the basic steps and view the task of calculation in its specific context, the job is not complicated.

■ THE IMPORTANCE OF LAND MEASUREMENT

As a starting point, why do you need to be able to measure land and building space? Many possible applications will arise during the course of looking at properties you are thinking about buying, calculating and comparing potential rental income on a size-specific basis, or checking the efficiency of cash flow.

Example: You are considering purchasing a triangular lot in a rural area. The property description identifies the property size as "5 to 6 acres." You make an offer, and it is accepted; however, you would like to know precisely how much land you are purchasing. The listing also supplies the number of feet for each of the three sides. With the ability to calculate the area of a triangle, you conclude that the land area is slightly more than 4.5 acres. As a result, you write up an amended offer for a reduced purchase price. Your reasoning: The offer was made based on the listing's claim that the land contained 5 to 6 acres, and it contained only 4.5.

Example: An agricultural area contains numerous storage silos, and you have an opportunity to purchase a piece of land containing four silos of various sizes. The numbers you are given estimating rental value are based on the amount of storage. To calculate this and to verify the claims made by the seller, you need to calculate the volume of each silo.

Example: You are thinking about purchasing several different properties. One listing provides a detailed description of a rectangular lot's measurements, but it does not provide total square feet. Knowing how to calculate the area of a rectangle enables you to figure out the total square feet, and you can then convert that to acreage.

Example: A rental property is set up as a shared house. Several college students split the cost of common areas and have individual rooms. You need to calculate (1) the overall area, (2) the proportion of the space each tenant occupies, and (3) the prorated responsibility for common areas.

Example: You are thinking about selling an investment property, but before proceeding, you would like to estimate the appraised value. Some local phone calls reveal the typical replacement cost per square foot. To get a fair estimate of the replacement cost for your property, you will need to measure the internal space.

These examples demonstrate that figuring out size, shape, and volume is not merely a theoretical issue or a topic that is of interest only to appraisers and lenders. In fact, every real estate investor will repeatedly run into situations in which these mathematical skills will be valuable. If you depend on the assurances of real estate agents or sellers, you may get estimates only or downright inaccurate information. Land value is estimated based on lot size. The value of improvements is calculated in many ways, and a common appraisal method is calculation of replacement cost, which is expressed in cost per square foot.

Even comparing the cash flow and investment value among several properties that you own or that you are considering buying requires calculations. Figuring out rent on the basis of square feet is a good way to make such comparisons, but that requires the ability to perform those basic calculations. In this chapter, you will find a range of formulas for measuring land area, internal space, and volume, for both standard shapes and odd shapes.

AREA AND PERIMETER

The starting point for most land measurements is figuring out the land's *perimeter*. This is the total size of the outer boundary of a shape. For example, a lot can be described as having a perimeter consisting of a series of measurements, one for each side. The perimeter may also be called the size of the edge, boundary, or property line. While perimeter describes the boundary, *area* is a precise measurement of the size within the shape.

The calculation of area varies with the shape itself. Calculating area for squares and rectangles is very simple, and this serves as the basis for figuring the area of more complex shapes. You need these because not all pieces of land are square or rectangular. Some lots are oddly shaped.

Formula: Area of a Square or Rectangle

$L \times W = A$

where L = length
W = width
A = area

The same formula can be used for either shape. For example, one piece of property is perfectly square, measuring 90 by 90 feet. Another is rectangular, measuring 80 by 110 feet. To calculate the area in square feet for each of these shapes,

$90 \times 90 = 8,100$ square feet
$80 \times 110 = 8,800$ square feet

Squares and rectangles may have additional variations, but with the same calculations. A *parallelogram* has opposite sides that are of equal length (a sort of slanted rectangle), and a *rhombus* is a type of parallelogram with equal sides that are not at right angles (like a slanted square). The area of all these shapes is calculated on the same basis, but because the shape of the parallelogram and rhombus involve distortion of two sides, the correct formula for these is *base* multiplied by *height*—rather than *length* multiplied by *width* in calculations of the square and rectangle. These shapes are illustrated in Figure 12.1.

It may also be necessary to convert measurements from other units into feet before making the calculation. Conversions between metric and U.S. measures are summarized in Appendix A. For converting from yards or inches to feet, it may be necessary to combine two separate conversion formulas.

Formula: Conversion, Yards to Feet

$Y \times 3 = F$

where Y = yards
      F = feet

Formula: Conversion, Inches to Feet

$$\frac{I}{12} = F$$

where I = inches
      F = feet

Example: You are given the measurements of a lot in yards and inches. The length is described as 12 yards, 22 inches; and the width is 11 yards, 4 inches. To convert these to feet:

Length:

    12 yards × 3 = 36 feet
    22 inches ÷ 12 = 1.83 feet
    Total feet: 36 + 1.83 = 37.83 feet

Width:

    11 yards × 3 = 33 feet
    4 inches ÷ 12 = 0.33 feet
    Total feet: 33 + 0.33 = 33.33 feet

Figure 12.1.   Square and Rectangular Shapes.

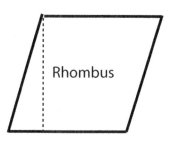

Area:

    37.83 × 33.33 = 1,260.87 square feet

The provision of land measurements in yards and inches may be unusual, as most measurements are expressed in feet or square feet. However, it is useful to be prepared for any required conversion task.

Land comes in all shapes and sizes, and measurements may be presented to you in various calculating systems. So it may also be necessary to convert square feet to acres, or vice versa. There are 43,560 square feet in one acre. Converting square feet to acreage requires division of the total number of square feet by the square feet in one acre.

Formula: Conversion, Square Feet to Acres

$$\frac{F}{43,560} = A$$

where F = square feet
      A = number of acres

For example, you previously calculated the size of a lot at 1,260.87 square feet. To calculate the same size in acres:

1,260.87 ÷ 43,560 = 0.029 acres, or 2.9% of one acre

If you need to convert in the opposite direction, you need to multiply the number of acres by 43,560.

Formula: Conversion, Acres to Square Feet

A × 43,560 = F

where A = acres
      F = square feet

For example, a seller is advertising a piece of land for sale. The size listed in the ad is 1.35 acres. Another ad lists the size of a lot as 3/4 of an acre (or 75 percent of one acre). To figure the square feet for each piece of land:

1.35 × 43,560 = 58,806 square feet
0.75 × 43,560 = 32,670 square feet

There are many practical applications of these basic land calculations. In order to compare the size of different properties, you need to know how to express varying measurements in the same way, so computation *and* conversion formulas are both necessary. You may also need to convert different calculating methods for one piece of property. This comes up when you need to compare several different properties in terms of both acreage and the *floor-area ratio*. This is a percentage-based comparison between a building's area and the total land area.

Example: You are thinking of making an offer on one of three different properties. Because you want to keep open the possibility of expanding the property later or selling off a portion of the land, you are looking at properties for sale with residential improvements and land. You find the following properties:

A: 2.7 acres and a 2,200-square-foot house
B: 3.0 acres and a 2,000-square-foot house
C: 3.3 acres and a 2,200-square-foot house

In order to compare floor-area ratios for each of these properties, two steps are required. First, you need to convert acres to square feet, using the formula previously introduced, $A \times 43,560 = F$:

A: 2.7 × 43,560 = 117,612
B: 3.0 × 43,560 = 130,680
C: 3.3 × 43,560 = 143,748

Next, you need to divide the building area by the land area.

Formula: Floor-Area Ratio

$$\frac{B}{L} = F$$

where B = building area
      L = land area
      F = floor-area ratio

There are four additional variations on measurement of area. The first is the *gross building area (GBA)*. This is a measurement of the exterior area of a building, without consideration for what is contained within it. For example, for a property measuring 43 feet by 50 feet (a straightforward rectangle), the gross building area is:

43 × 50 = 2,150 square feet

This is the basic rectangle formula for figuring area. It becomes more complex when you deal with a building that has variations in shape or multiple stories.

For example, look at Figure 12.2. This is an example of a building whose area cannot be calculated using the rectangular formula alone. The outer area is 40 × 60 feet, or 2,400 total square feet; however, an indented area measures 10 × 10 feet, or 100 square feet. In this case, the area can be easily adjusted by deducting 100 from the gross area and concluding that the GBA is actually 2,300 square feet.

The calculation may be more complex when a series of outer-wall changes are involved. You may need to calculate several additions to or subtractions from the initial calculation or make a series of smaller area calculations. Returning to Figure 12.2, you could also divide this property into three sections: the upper left section, measuring 30 × 10 feet; the lower left section, measuring 20 × 10 feet; and the right-hand section, a rectangle measuring 30 × 60 feet:

```
30 × 10 =    300
20 × 10 =    200
30 × 60 = 1,800
Total      2,300
```

The result is the same. This approach will be appropriate when the number of variations in outer size makes using the first method by itself too complex.

Figure 12.2.   Odd-Shaped Building Area.

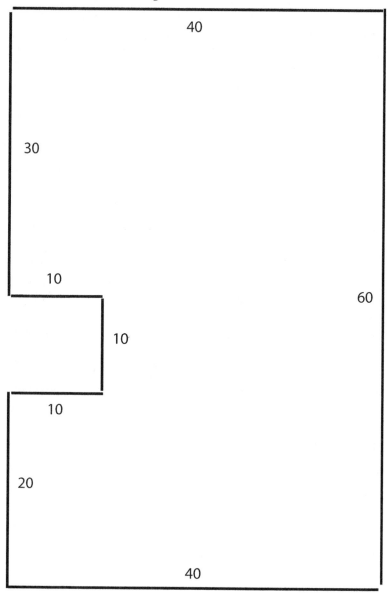

You may also need to calculate *usable square footage*, which is a valuable comparative tool. This is a ratio used in commercial property analysis or in multifamily buildings, where some parts of the interior of the building are not available. For example, a building may contain six separate units, with wall and utility space in between.

When a property includes numerous units and nonrental space, the calculation of usable space can become complex. It may seem a minor point, but when added together, the combined nonusable areas can become a significant portion of the total building's area.

The tendency to calculate these areas' sizes may complicate the rental issues. In other words, the calculation of how much rent to charge can be vastly simplified by simply calculating the square feet of each unit and determining fair market rent based on unit area. A comparison to other properties, or even to classified ads, provides a fair and reasonable estimate of what you can charge for a space. If the typical 400-foot unit goes for $550 per month, and the typical 600-foot unit commands $700 in rents, you can calculate the relative value of units without needing to also look at nonusable space. It makes sense to simplify your calculations. As long as you know how much rent you need to generate for a building, you can easily prorate the total based on rental area. For example, if you need to generate $2,000 per month and your building has three units (with square feet of 400, 550, and 575 feet), you can prorate the $2,000 total by unit. Total square adds up to 1,575, so the units' percentages are 26 percent, 36 percent and 38 percent (rounded). And your rents should be $520 (26 percent × $2,000); $720 (36 percent × $2,000); and $760 (38 percent × $2,000).

The calculation of nonusable square feet is more important for comparisons between properties and an analysis of efficiency in a building's space. You pay for the whole building, even when a portion cannot be rented out. So if one building has about 8 percent nonusable space and another has 16 percent, the second building provides far less efficiency, 84 percent rental space versus 92 percent for the first one. For example, if you estimate that market rents are approximately $1.30 per square foot of rental space, the nonusable space becomes an important factor. In a building with a total of 1,800 feet, a nonusable total of 16 percent (288 feet) represents reduced rents of $374 per month). If a comparable building of the same overall size has only 8 percent nonusable space (144 feet), the lost rent is half, or about $187.

Considering that cash flow is usually a very critical issue for rental properties (not to mention maximizing value by also maximizing rental income), the nonusable space may be very significant when determining which building to purchase. The feasibility of the rental property is going to be determined by design efficiency. You cannot simply raise rents to make up for the inefficiency in design; you will need to conform to a range of market rates.

The immediate cash flow is only one of two concerns. The second is market value of the property itself. By definition, nonusable space is valueless. When you want to sell your property, its value will be determined by market rents and, in practice, market rates are determined by rental square feet and not by total square feet. So if nonusable space is equal to 16 percent of the total area, whereas another building's is only 8 percent, then your building will have *twice as much* valueless space.

This does not mean that in all cases it is fair or realistic to ignore nonusable space in calculating rents. This space should be classified in two ways. First is the space that has no aesthetic value to renters, such as utility space, internal systems, and walls. Second is the common area space, which is not actually nonusable. Consider the difference in rental attractiveness between a two-story building. The ground floor has street-level doorway access but the second floor includes a foyer, staircase, and hallways. Those areas may serve as gathering places, out-of-unit but usable areas, and areas that add value to the units. In these situations, it is fair and reasonable to add some extra rental to the upstairs units. The method is one of individual choice, however. It may not be fair to charge the same per-foot value for common areas, but clearly, the units with access to those additional areas should pay more per square foot than the units lacking the same features. A similar problem arises when you consider access to porch or yard areas. In the same building, for example, the ground-level porch and fenced yard features may offset the foyer and hallway amenities of upper units. In all instances such as these, you will need to make value judgments and adjust rents based on what the market will bear. The cost per square foot is not ironclad, but has to be adjusted upward for conveniences and downward for what units may lack. That price per square foot could be based on availability (or lack) of washer and dryer, transportation, or other features (noise levels, traffic, density).

The point is, there is no universally used standard for calculating *rentable square feet*. In cases where market rates are expressed in terms of unit size, it may be critical to include common areas such as hallways and to ignore the space taken up by interior and exterior walls, laundry rooms, and other nonrentable space. In the previous example, the unusable area was the size of a 500-square-foot apartment, so the difference can be substantial. Looking at the drawing of the fourplex, you might not realize how much area is involved in this, and while the illustration simplified the measurements to make the point, a landlord might advertise these units as containing 520 square feet (units 1 and 2) and 400 square feet (units 3 and 4) or, more realistically, as containing the net of 428 and 320 square feet. For example, let's assume that the advertised rentable area is based on the exterior of the building rather than on the actual interior square feet. In this situation, the hallway common area is split about equally and you could simply use an approximation. So this complex may be said to contain four units, two measuring 520 square feet and two measuring 400 square feet. The explanation that common areas and unusable areas are counted as part of the total is acceptable as long as the standard is used consistently. You also assume that tenants recognize the inclusion of area that is not available to them. Smart tenants may actually measure the interior usable space to make their own comparisons between available units.

Finally, the *loss ratio* reveals the number of square feet in a building that cannot be rented out. This is also a valuable comparative calculation owing to the fact that building designs differ. Two buildings with identical gross building area may contain different rentable areas because of hallway and corridor configurations, laundry rooms, lobbies, stairways and elevators, heating and cooling equipment areas, common storage rooms, and, of course, interior walls.

In multiunit residential buildings (as well as in commercial rentals), owners may compute the relationship between net rentable area and gross building area and subsequently charge tenants a proportionate additional rent for the portion represented in the loss ratio.

Formula: Loss Ratio

$$\frac{N}{G} = L$$

where N = nonrentable area
      G = gross building area
      L = loss ratio

ADVANCED CALCULATIONS

Figuring area for square and rectangular shapes is not complex. Unfortunately, land does not always come in these simple shapes. Some land is triangular or oddly shaped. In some types of land calculations, you may even need to calculate the area of a circle. For example, if you are calculating a crop yield for land that is farmed in a circular pattern because of the available watering system, it would not be accurate to count the square acreage, since actual yield will be less. You may also need to calculate the volume of buildings of different shapes. If you want to know the storage capacity of a silo, which is a cylinder, you need to know how to figure that capacity.

Triangles present a particular challenge because they contain three sides rather than four, and they come in different forms. An *equilateral triangle* has three sides that are exactly equal in length. Another type of triangle has two equal sides and a third side of a different length. And a third type of triangle has three sides, all of which are different in length.

A starting point for calculating the area of a triangle is calculating the number of feet for each of the sides. You should not be as concerned with angles for this discussion, because for land investors, the emphasis is invariably on the amount of land involved. To calculate area, you need to know two measurements: *base* and *altitude*. The base is any of the sides of the triangle, and the altitude is the shortest distance from the base to the point where the other

two sides meet. This is illustrated in Figure 12.4 for all three variations of the triangle.

In any of the three variations of triangular shape, area is figured
by multiplying the base by the altitude and dividing the result by 2.

Formula: Area of a Triangle

$$\frac{b \times a}{2} = A$$

where b = base
       a = altitude
       A = area of a triangle

(*Note:* In calculations involving triangles, lowercase designa-
tions are used for base and altitude. Uppercase letters are reserved
for identifying the *angles* of triangles, and lowercase letters are consistently used for the length of the sides. Lowercase letters are also
used in calculations for some other shapes as well.)

You can also use altitude in figuring the area of a *trapezoid*.
This shape contains four sides, of which at least two are of different
lengths, as illustrated in Figure 12.5.

Figure 12.4.   Base and Altitude of Triangles.

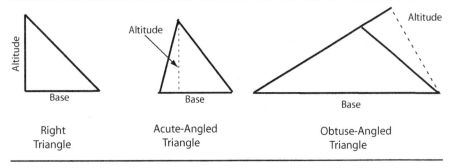

| Right Triangle | Acute-Angled Triangle | Obtuse-Angled Triangle |

Figure 12.5.   The Trapezoid.

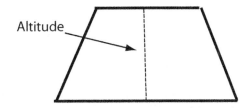

To calculate the area of a trapezoid, you add together the two bases (top and bottom lengths) and divide the sum by 2, and then multiply that answer by the altitude.

Formula: Area of a Trapezoid

$$\frac{b_1 + b_2}{2} \times a = A$$

where b_1 = base number 1
b_2 = base number 2
a = altitude
A = area of a trapezoid

It may be necessary to combine the calculations for squares with those for triangles to calculate the area of odd-shaped lots. For example, you may need to break down an odd-shaped lot into a rectangle and one or more triangles, calculate the area of each part, and then add them together.

A different approach is required in calculating the *area of a circle*. The outer line is called the *circumference*, and the *diameter* is a straight line from any point on the circle through the middle to the opposite side. The *radius* is a straight line from any point on the circumference, to the exact middle point of the circle. When circles are perfect, calculations of area are not complex; but when a segment of a circle is excluded, the computation is far more complex (and beyond the scope of this book). We limit our calculations to situations like the one previously described, such as needing to know the area of a circular piece of agricultural land that is shaped that way because of a watering system.

To figure the area of a circle, you need to employ the value of *pi*. This is the 16th letter of the Greek alphabet, and it is used in mathematical formulas to denote the value of circumference divided by diameter. No matter what the size of a circle may be, pi is always the same. Pi is denoted using the Greek letter π.

Formula: Pi

$$\frac{C}{D} = \pi$$

where C = circumference of a circle
D = diameter of a circle
π = value of pi, ~3.1416

While many uses of pi or approximations to it have been used throughout history—including estimates in the Bible[1]—the first approximation in mathematical form is credited to Archimedes (287–212 BC). His formula is called an approximation because pi is not an exact value. Archimedes summarized pi as:

$$223 \div 71 < \pi < 22 \div 7$$

Recognizing that pi does not have an exact value, most calculations can dependably be made using 3.1416. This is a midpoint between the two sides of Archimedes' equation. The decimal equivalent of $223 \div 71$ is 3.1408. And the decimal equivalent of $22 \div 7$ is 3.1429. So the formula states that 3.1408 is less than pi, which is less than 3.1429.

All of this is important because you need the approximate value of pi to find the *area of a circle*. The formula involves squaring the radius and multiplying the result by pi.

Formula: Area of a Circle

$$\pi \times r^2 = A$$

where π = pi
   r = radius
   A = area of a circle

For example, if the radius of a circular piece of land (the distance from the circumference to the exact middle of the circle, or one-half the diameter) is 82 feet, the area is:

$$3.1416 \times 82^2 = 21,124.12 \text{ square feet}$$

One final type of measurement that real estate investors may need in some circumstances is *volume*. This has several possible applications. Appraisals of some property may be performed on the basis of volume, or the size within a three-dimensional shape (a cube or a cylinder, for example). You need two basic formulas, one

---

[1] "And he made a molten sea, ten cubits from the one brim to the other: it was round all about, and his height was five cubits: and a line of thirty cubits did compass it about." (I Kings 7: 23)

for the volume of a rectangular solid (including squares and rectangles) and one for the volume of a cylinder (such as a grain silo, for example).

The *volume of a rectangular solid* is an expansion of the linear land area. Volume adds a third dimension because land measurement involves only length and width. Volume also includes height.

Formula: Volume of a Rectangular Solid

$L \times W \times H = V$

where L = length
       W = width
       H = height
       V = volume

For example, suppose you are comparing prices for industrial warehouse storage facilities. For such properties, internal storage height is an important valuation feature, so you make your comparison based on a measurement of volume rather than using only floor space. You are reviewing three buildings, and their measurements are length, width, and height:

A: $90 \times 85 \times 24 = 183,600$
B: $105 \times 60 \times 30 = 189,000$
C: $115 \times 75 \times 18 = 155,250$

In this comparison, the third building would appear to have the largest area based on length and width, but when the relatively low height is considered, is becomes clear that the volume for the first two buildings is more desirable—at least in terms of storage capacity related to height itself. So if storage capacity is more significant in deciding between properties, the calculation of comparative volume is crucial to making an informed decision.

To calculate the volume of a cylinder, combine the calculation of the area of a circle with the height. To do this, multiply pi times the square of the radius *and* the height.

Formula: Volume of a Cylinder

$\pi \times r^2 \times H = V$

where π = pi
     r = radius
     H = height
     V = volume

▪ LAND MEASUREMENT STANDARDS

Knowing how to calculate the area or volume for any size of lot or building is a necessary skill. In reviewing legal descriptions of land or comparing building and land sizes between different properties, you also need to be aware of the different systems in use for describing land.

The system that has been in use for the longest time is called *metes and bounds*. This is a good system for accurately describing land with an irregular shape, as is often the case. Metes and bounds begin at a specific starting point (a monument or known landmark) and identify the precise direction and length of each piece of a property's perimeter, always ending up at the *point of beginning*. Calculations of metes and bounds are based on the *azimuth system* and on the *bearing system* for identifying direction. This is necessary because boundary lines do not always run exactly north, south, east, and west. Actual boundary lines may have any number of degrees in between those exact directions.

The azimuth system is a method for identifying compass direction based on a circle in which north is at the top. In using this system to calculate metes and bounds, the readings always begin at the northernmost boundary and move clockwise. Because a circle contains 360 degrees, due south would be 180 degrees, due east would be 90 degrees, and due west would be 270 degrees. The eight major divisions of the circle are summarized in Figure 12.6.

Of course, there are any number of angles in between these major eight points. Using the azimuth system, the direction of the property line is described in terms of a specific angle.

Under the *bearing system*, the circle is divided into four parts, and each direction is described as having a precise bearing. The four *quadrants* of the circle are northeast (NE), southeast (SE), southwest (SW), and northwest (NW). In writing down a bearing, three parts are included: the first letter indicating the direction (N, E, S, or W); the degrees, minutes, and seconds; and the second

Figure 12.6.   Degrees of a Circle.

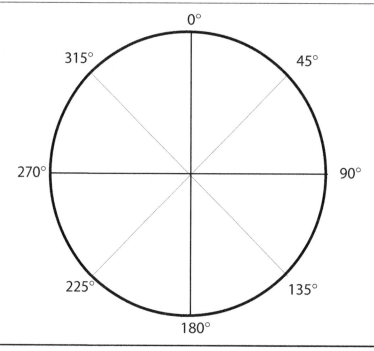

letter within the quadrant (E or W). For example, a bearing description reading N 80° 20′ 32″ E precisely describes a line's direction at an angle moving eastward and rising at a specific angle;
next, the description would describe the exact number of feet the
line travels in that direction.

The United States Geological Survey (USGS) system is also
known as the grid system and is used to describe land boundaries
in surveys. This system consists of a north-south line called a *principal meridian* and an east-west line called a *baseline*. Additional
lines run parallel to each of these, placed at intervals of 24 miles
in either direction. These are referred to as *guide meridians* and
correction lines. The 24-mile squares that result are called *checks*
or *quadrangles*.

Dividing these squares into smaller tracts at six-mile intervals
are *range lines*; these define smaller groupings of square land areas
called *townships*. A township's north-south line is called a *range*,
and the east-west line is called a *tier*. This system leads to the label-
ing of areas by specific location, so on plat maps, an area can be

described by township number and by range, such as "Township 3 North, Range 2 West," which tells you exactly where the land is located on a map that is labeled and numbered.

Figure 12.7 provides an example of the USGS system showing these various lines and their names.

Under this system, every quadrangle contains 16 townships, each 6 miles square in size. Each of these townships is further divided into 36 smaller squares, each 1 mile square in size. These units are called *sections*. They can be further divided into subsections of 40 acres. These can be even further broken down into individual tracts.

A final breakdown of land is the lot and block system. When

Figure 12.7.   USGS Land Line System.

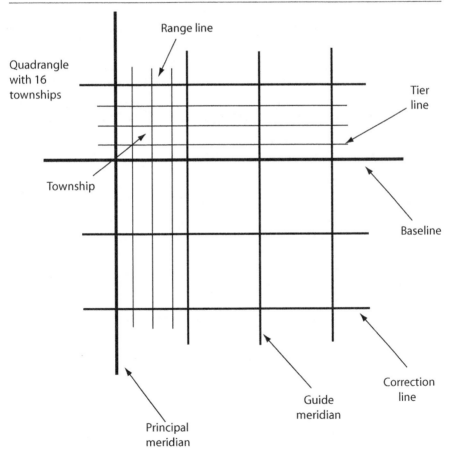

property within a city or town is described, a lot number is usually further identified as belonging to a tract, which in turn is found within a section. Tracts are broken down into smaller blocks, and those blocks are divided into lots. Each of these distinct units of land is given a number, so that a plat map identifies a specific property in terms of size, shape, and ownership. Legal descriptions may identify a piece of land is "lot 4, block 1, tract 17 of plat 42." This tells you exactly which piece of land is involved. Or a legal description may involve metes and bounds and describe the property exactly, giving the starting point and the compass degrees and number of feet for each turn.

While precise calculations of land are going to be more complex for odd-shaped lots than for simple squares or rectangles, the exact calculations are not difficult to master. Applying these calculations to a completely platted map further aids in describing land, so that buyers, sellers, assessors, and real estate salespeople can all agree on where land is located, and on its exact size.

Do real estate investors need to become expert mathematicians? No, but they do need to be able to employ a variety of formulas, used for many different reasons. The more capable you are in applying these calculations, the better your decision making regarding real estate investments will be.

CONVERSION

SIMPLE RULES, EASY ANSWERS

CONVERSIONS BETWEEN VARYING SYSTEMS, or between different methods of measuring distance or area within a single system, can be done by referring to conversion tables or finding online calculators.

Online calculators are normally free and easy to use. A search will locate numerous tables and automatic calculator programs available to everyone.

Valuable resource:

For a range of conversion formulas, search online under "metric conversion." One very easy to use site is located at http://www.sciencemade simple.com/conversions.html.

The following conversion tables present the level of measurement conversions you are most likely to encounter in measurements relating to real estate. Accordingly, we exclude very large and very small measurements because it is unlikely that they will be useful.

The *metric system* is based on divisions and multiples of 10. The precise level of division is determined by the prefix:

kilo-	=	1,000
hecto-	=	100
deca-	=	10
	=	1
deci-	=	0.1
centi-	=	0.01
milli	=	0.001

Following are tables for converting distance, area, and volume.

DISTANCE

The first table shows a comparison from metric to U.S. equivalents:

Metric Value Conversions

Unit	Symbol	Number of Meters	Approximate Distance in U.S. Measurement
Kilometer	km	1,000	0.62 mile
Hectometer	hm	100	328.08 feet
Decameter	dam	10	32.81 feet
Meter	m	1	39.37 inches
Decimeter	dm	0.1	3.94 inches
Centimeter	cm	0.01	0.39 inch
Millimeter	mm	0.001	0.039 inch

The second table summarizes conversion back and forth between the metric and U.S. systems and within the U.S. system.

Conversion Table by Type and Size Ranges

1 inch	= 2.54 centimeters
1 foot	= 0.3048 meter
1 yard	= 0.9144 meter
1 yard	= 0.5 fathom
1 yard	= 36 inches
1 yard	= 3 feet

1 mile*	= 1.60934 kilometers
1 mile	= 5,280 feet
1 mile	= 0.8684 nautical mile
1 nautical mile	= 1.1516 miles (statute miles)
1 rod	= 5.029 meters
1 rod	= 5.5 yards
1 rod	= 16.5 feet
1 furlong	= 0.125 mile
1 furlong	= 40 rods
1 furlong	= 660 feet

1 millimeter	= 0.03937 inch
1 centimeter	= 0.3937 inch
1 centimeter	= 0.03281 foot
1 centimeter	= 0.01094 yard

1 meter	= 39.37 inches
1 meter	= 3.281 feet
1 meter	= 1.094 yards

1 kilometer	= 3,280.84 feet
1 kilometer	= 1,094 yards
1 kilometer	= 0.6214 mile

AREA

The first table shows a comparison from metric units to their U.S. equivalents.

Metric Value Conversions

Unit	Symbol	Number of Square Meters	Approximate Size in U.S. Measurement
Square kilometer	km²	1,000,000	0.3861 square miles
Hectare	ha	10,000	2.47 acres
Are	a	100	119.60 square yards
Square centimeter	cm²	0.0001	0.155 square inch

The second table summarizes conversion back and forth between the metric and U.S. systems and within the U.S. system.

---

* "Mile" refers to *statute mile* unless nautical mile is specified.

Conversion Table by Type and Area Range

1 square inch	= 6.452 square centimeters
1 square foot	= 144 square inches
1 square foot	= 0.1111 square yard
1 square foot	= 0.0929 square meter
1 square yard	= 9 square feet
1 square mile	= 2.59 square kilometers
1 square mile	= 640 acres
1 acre	= 160 square rods
1 acre	= 0.04047 hectare (square hectometer)
1 acre	= 43,560 square feet
1 acre	= 4,840 square yards
1 acre	= 0.001562 square mile
1 acre	= 4,047 square meters
1 square centimeter	= 0.155 square inch
1 square meter	= 1.196 square yards
1 square kilometer	= 0.3861 square mile
1 square kilometer	= 247.1 acres
1 hectare	= 2.471 acres

VOLUME

The first table shows a comparison from metric units to their U.S. equivalents.

Unit	Symbol	Number of Cubic Meters	Approximate Size in U.S. Measurement
Cubic meter	m³	1	1.307 cubic yards
Cubic decimeter	dm³	0.001	61.023 cubic inches
Cubic centimeter	cm³ or cc	0.00000	0.061 cubic inch

The second table summarizes conversion back and forth between the metric and U.S. systems and within the U.S. system.

Conversion Table by Type and Volume Range

1 cubic foot	= 1,728 cubic inches
1 cubic foot	= 0.037037037 cubic yard
1 cubic foot	= 0.02832 cubic meter
1 cubic yard	= 27 cubic feet
1 cubic yard	= 0.7646 cubic meter
1 cubic meter	= 35.31 cubic feet
1 cubic meter	= 1.307951 cubic yards

A P P E N D I X   B

REAL ESTATE FORMULAS

SUMMARIZING THE ESSENTIALS

Accelerated Depreciation

$$\frac{B}{P} \times R = D$$

where B = basis of asset
      P = period (in years)
      R = acceleration rate
      D = annual depreciation

Accumulated Value

$(R + 1)^n \times P = A$

where R = periodic interest rate
      n = periods
      P = principal amount
      A = amount accumulated (principal plus interest)

Accumulated Value per Period

$$D\left[\frac{(1 + R)^n - 1)}{R}\right] \times P = A$$

where D = periodic deposit amount
      R = periodic interest rate
      n = number of periods
      P = principal
      A = accumulated value of 1

Actual Percentage Rate

$$\left[\left(\frac{i}{P}\right) + 1\right]^n - 1 = R$$

where i = annual interest rate
      P = number of periods
      n = number of periods in a full year
      R = periodic interest rate

Adjusted Basis in Property

$(P + C = A) - D = B$

where P = purchase price
      C = closing costs
      A = adjusted purchase price
      D = deferred gain
      B = basis in property

Adjusted Purchase Price

$P + C = A$

where P = purchase price
      C = closing costs
      A = adjusted purchase price

Adjusted Sales Price

$S - C = A$

where S = sales price
      C = closing costs
      A = adjusted sales price

After-Tax Cash Flow

$[R - (E + D)] - (P + C - T) = CF$

where R   = rental income
      E   = cash expenses
      D   = depreciation
      P   = principal payments
      C   = capital expenditures
      T   = income tax savings
      CF = after-tax cash flow

Amortization Payment

$$B\left(\frac{1}{P^n}\right) = A$$

where B = balance of the loan
      P = present value of 1 per period
      n = number of periods
      A = amount of payment per period

Annual Compounding

$(R + 1)^y = i$

where R $=$ interest rate
      y $=$ number of years
      i $=$ accumulated interest

Annualized Return (Using Months)

$(R \div H) \times 12 = A$

where R $=$ return over entire holding period
      H $=$ holding period (number of months)
      A $=$ annualized return

Annualized Return (Using Years)

$$\frac{R}{H} = A$$

where R $=$ return over entire holding period
      H $=$ holding period (number of years)
      A $=$ annualized return

Area of a Circle

$\pi \times r^2 = A$

where π $=$ pi
      r $=$ radius
      A $=$ area of a circle

Area of a Square or Rectangle

$L \times W = A$

where L $=$ length
      W $=$ width
      A $=$ area

Area of a Trapezoid

$$\frac{b_1 + b_2}{2} \times a = A$$

where b_1 $=$ base number 1
      b_2 $=$ base number 2
      a $=$ altitude
      A $=$ area of a trapezoid

Area of a Triangle

$$\frac{b \times a}{2} = A$$

where b = base
  a = altitude
  A = area of a triangle

Assessment Ratio

$$\frac{P}{A} = R$$

where P = asked price
  A = assessed value
  R = assessment ratio

Assessment Ratio Adjusted

$$\frac{P(1 + i)^y}{A} = R$$

where P = asked price
  i = average annual increase in assessed value
  y = years since last assessment
  A = assessed value
  R = assessment ratio

Balance Sheet

$$A = L + N$$

where A = assets
  L = liabilities
  N = net worth

Bank Reconciliation

$$(C + (-)E) = A = (B + T - O + (-)E)$$

where C = checkbook balance
  E = errors
  A = reconciled balance
  B = bank statement balance
  T = deposits in transit
  O = outstanding checks

Breakeven After Taxes and Inflation

$$\frac{I}{100 - E} = B$$

where I = inflation rate
       E = effective tax rate
       B = breakeven after taxes and inflation

Breakeven Ratio

$$\frac{O + M}{G} = R$$

where O = operating expenses
      M = mortgage debt service
      G = effective gross income
      R = breakeven ratio

Breakeven Ratio Net of Taxes

$$\frac{O + M - [(O + I + D) \times E]}{G} = R$$

where O = operating expenses
      M = mortgage debt service
      I = interest
      D = depreciation
      E = effective tax rate
      G = effective gross income
      R = breakeven ratio net of taxes

Capital Gain or Loss

$$(S - C) - L + D - (P - C - G) = N$$

where S = sale price
      C = closing costs
      L = carryover losses
      D = depreciation claimed
      P = purchase price
      G = deferred gains
      N = net capital gain or loss

Capitalization Rate

$$\frac{I}{P} = C$$

where I = annual net income
      P = purchase price
      C = capitalization rate

Carryover Loss Allocation

$$\frac{L}{T} = A$$

where L = loss reported for the property
T = total net loss, all properties
A = allocation percentage

Cash Income

$$N + D = C$$

where N = net income
D = depreciation expense
C = cash income

Cash-on-Cash Return

$$\frac{C}{I} = R$$

where C = annual cash flow
I = cash invested
R = cash-on-cash return

Checking Account Math Verification

$$E + C - D = P$$

where E = ending balance
C = checks
D = deposits
P = previous balance

Closing Prorated Days (Buyer)

$$R - D = P$$

where R = days remaining as of prior month-end
D = days in partial month
P = prorated days, buyer

Closing Prorated Days (Seller)

$$U + D = P$$

where U = days used as of prior month-end
D = days in partial month
P = prorated days, seller

Closing Prorated Interest

$$\frac{L \times I}{12} \times \frac{D}{M} = P$$

where L = loan amount
     I = interest rate
     D = days of prorated interest
     M = days in the month
     P = prorated interest

Closing Prorated Property Taxes

$$T \times \frac{D}{L} = P$$

where T = total property tax bill, half-year
     D = days of responsibility
     L = days in liability period
     P = prorated property taxes

Conversion, Acres to Square Feet

$$A \times 43{,}560 = F$$

where A = acres
     F = square feet

Conversion, Inches to Feet

$$\frac{I}{12} = F$$

where I = inches
     F = feet

Conversion, Percentage to Decimal

$$\frac{R}{100} = D$$

where R = interest rate
     D = decimal equivalent

Conversion, Square Feet to Acres

$$\frac{F}{43{,}560} = A$$

where F = square feet
     A = acres

Conversion, Yards to Feet

$Y \times 3 = F$

where Y = yards
F = feet

Cost Approach

$C - D + L = V$

where C = cost of improvements
D = depreciation
L = land value
V = value of the property

Cost of Financed Property

$(P \times M) + D = C$

where P = monthly payment
M = number of months in loan term
D = down payment
C = total cost of property

Cost per Unit

$V \times U = C$

where V = average value per unit
U = number of units
C = cost per unit

Current Ratio

$$\frac{A}{L} = R$$

where A = current assets
L = current liabilities
R = current ratio

Current Yield (Bond)

$$\frac{NY}{PD} = Y$$

where NY = nominal yield
PD = premium or discount
Y = current yield

Current Yield (Stock)

$$\frac{D}{P} = Y$$

where D = dividend per share
       P = current price per share
       Y = current yield

Daily Compounding

$$\frac{R}{365} = i$$

where R = annual interest rate
      i = daily rate

Debt coverage ratio

$$\frac{I}{M} = R$$

where I = net operating income
     M = mortgage payment
     R = debt coverage ratio

Depreciation (Appraisal)

$$\frac{100}{E} = D$$

where E = economic life
     D = annual rate of depreciation

Depreciation Basis (Appraised Value)

$$\frac{I}{V} = A$$

where I = improvement value per appraisal
     V = total appraised value
     A = allocated basis, improvements

Depreciation Basis (Assessed Value)

$$\frac{I}{V} = A$$

where I = improvement value per assessment
     V = total assessed value
     A = allocated basis, improvements

Depreciation Basis (Insured Value)

$$\frac{L}{V} = A$$

where L = insurance limits of liability, dwelling
      V = total basis in the property
      A = allocated basis, improvements

Discount Yield

$$\frac{A - P}{A} = Y$$

where A = appraised value
      P = asked price
      Y = discount yield

Double-Entry Bookkeeping, Basic Formula

$$D = C$$

where D = balance of all debit-balance accounts
      C = balance of all credit-balance accounts

Economic Rent per Room

$$\frac{R}{N} = E$$

where R = rent per period
      N = number of rooms
      E = economic rent per room

Economic Rent per Square Foot

$$\frac{R}{S} = E$$

where R = rent per period
      S = square feet
      E = economic rent per square foot

Economic Rent per Unit

$$\frac{R}{U} = E$$

where R = rent per period
      U = number of units
      E = economic rent per unit

Equity

$$V - B = E$$

where V = current market value
      B = balance, mortgage debt
      E = equity

Equity Dividend Yield

$$\frac{C}{D} = Y$$

where C = net cash flow
      D = down payment
      Y = equity dividend yield

Equity Return

$$\frac{C + P}{D} = R$$

where C = net cash income
      P = principal reduction
      D = down payment
      R = equity return

Estimated Monthly Payment

$$\frac{P_a + P_b}{N} = A$$

where P_a = payment, higher interest rate
      P_b = payment, lower interest rate
      N = number of rates
      A = average

Exercise Cost (to Owner)

$$\frac{(M - P) - O}{P} = C$$

where M = current market value
      P = fixed option price of the property
      O = option cost
      C = exercise cost

Exercise Return (to Tenant)

$$\frac{O}{M - P} = R$$

where O = option cost
      M = current market value
      P = fixed option price of property
      R = exercise return

Expense Allocation (Even Distribution)

$$\frac{E}{P} = A$$

where E = nonspecific expenses
      P = number of properties
      A = allocation percentage

Expense Allocation (Months Owned)

$$\frac{M}{E} = A$$

where M = months of ownership during the year
      T = total months of ownership, all properties
      A = allocation percentage

Expense Allocation (Prepayments)

$$\frac{E}{M} = A$$

where E = total prepaid expense
      M = number of months the expense relates to
      A = allocation amount

Expense Allocation (Revenue Share)

$$\frac{R}{T} = A$$

where R = revenue received for the property
      T = total revenue, all properties
      A = allocation percentage

Expense Allocation (Square Feet)

$$\frac{F}{T} = A$$

where F = rentable square feet, each unit
      T = total square feet, all units
      A = allocation percentage

Expense Ratio

$$\frac{E}{I} = R$$

where E = operating expenses
      I = gross income from rents
      R = expense ratio

Exponential Moving Average

$$\left(\frac{V_1 + V_2 + \cdots V_f}{N} - L \right) \times \frac{2}{N} + \frac{V_1 + V_2 + \cdots V_f}{N} = NA$$

where V   = values in the selected field
      1, 2, ... f = first, second, remaining, and final values
      N   = number of values in the field
      L   = latest entry
      NA   = new moving average

Floor-Area Ratio

$$\frac{B}{L} = F$$

where B = building area
      L = land area
      F = floor-area ratio

Gross Rent Multiplier

$$\frac{S}{R} = G$$

where S = sales price
      R = rent per period
      G = gross rent multiplier

Half-Year Convention

$$\frac{B}{2} = H$$

where B = basis of the asset
      H = half-year depreciation base, first year

Income Statement

$$R - (C + E) = N$$

where R = revenues
      C = costs
      E = general expenses
      N = net profit or loss

Loan-to-Value Ratio

$$\frac{L}{V} = R$$

where L = loan balance
      V = value (sales price or appraisal)
      R = ratio

Loss Ratio

$$\frac{N}{G} = L$$

where N = nonrentable area
      G = gross building area
      L = loss ratio

Market or Sales Comparison Approach

$$\left(\frac{C_1 + C_2 + \cdots C_n}{N} \right) \pm A = V$$

where C   = comparable property values
      1, 2 . . . n = comparable properties
      N   = average comparable values
      A   = plus or minus adjustments
      V   = market value

Math Check, Change in Loan Balance

$$PB - NB = P$$

where PB = previous balance, mortgage loan
      NB = new balance, mortgage loan
      P = principal payments

Math Check, Interest/Principal

P + I = T

where P = principal amounts
     I = interest amounts
     T = total of payments

Maximum Loss Allowance

$$\$25,000 - \frac{A - \$100,000}{2} = L$$

where A = adjusted gross income
     L = maximum loss allowed

Mid-Month Convention

$$\left(\frac{B}{24}\right) \times P = M$$

where B = basis of the asset
     P = number of half-month periods
     M = mid-month depreciation base, first year

Monthly Compounding

$$\frac{R}{12} = i$$

where R = interest rate
     i = monthly rate

Monthly Loan Amortization

PB − {T − [PB × (i ÷ 12)]} = NB

where PB = previous balance, mortgage loan
     T = total payment
     i = interest rate
     N = new balance, mortgage loan

Months of Property Inventory on the Market

$$\frac{I}{S} = M$$

where I = total inventory of properties currently available
     S = average sales per month
     M = months of inventory currently available

Moving Average

$$\frac{V_1 + V_2 + \cdots V_f}{N} = A$$

where V   = values in the selected field
      1, 2, . . . f = first, second, remaining, and final values
      N   = number of values in the field
      A   = moving average

Net Current Value of Property

$$C - (C \times R \times E) = N$$

where C = cost
      R = rate of depreciation
      E = effective age
      N = net current value

New Basis in 1031 Exchange

$$P - D = N$$

where P = adjusted purchase price
      D = deferred gain
      N = new basis

Occupancy Rate

$$\frac{O}{T} = R$$

where O = occupied units
      T = total units
      R = occupancy rate

Operating Expense Ratio

$$\frac{E}{I} = R$$

where E = operating expenses
      I = rental income
      R = operating expense ratio

Option to Exercise Ratio

$$\frac{O}{S} = R$$

where O = option price
      S = sale price upon exercise
      R = ratio

Partial Month's Rent Liability

$$\frac{D}{M} = P$$

where D = days in period to be counted
     M = full month
     P = partial month liability

Payback ratio

$$\frac{I}{C} = R$$

where I = investment
     C = net cash flow
     R = payback ratio

Periodic Rate

$$\frac{R}{P} = i$$

where R = annual interest rate
     P = number of periods
     i = periodic interest rate

Pi

$$\frac{C}{D} = \pi$$

where C = circumference of a circle
     D = diameter of a circle
     π = value of pi, ~3.1416

Present Value

$$\frac{1}{(1 + R)^n} = P$$

where R = periodic interest rate
     n = periods
     P = present value factor

Present Value per Period

$$\left[1 - \frac{1}{(1 + R)^n} \right] \div R = W$$

where R = periodic interest rate
       n = periods
      W = withdrawal amount

Profit Margin

$$\frac{C}{I} = P$$

where C = cash flow
       I = effective gross income
      P = profit margin

Prorated Rent, Partial-Year Use

$$\frac{R}{F} = P$$

where R = rental period
      F = full year
      P = prorated rent

Prorated Rent, Tenant Share

$$\frac{T}{F} = P$$

where T = tenant's square-foot share
      F = total square feet
      P = prorated rent

Quarterly Compounding

$$\frac{R}{4} = i$$

where R = interest rate
      i = quarterly rate

Rate of Return

$$\frac{V - C}{C} = R$$

where V = current value (or sales price)
      C = original cost or basis
      R = rate of return

Return on Equity

$$\frac{P - E}{E} = R$$

where P = proceeds upon sale
      E = equity (net market value minus debt)
      R = return on equity

Return on Investment

$$\frac{P - O}{O} = R$$

where P = proceeds upon sale
      O = original investment
      R = return on investment

Return on Rental Income

$$\frac{N}{I} = R$$

where N = net profit
      I = rental gross income (revenues)
      R = return on rental income

Rule of 69

$$\frac{69}{i} + 0.35 = Y$$

where i = interest rate
      Y = years required to double

Rule of 72

$$\frac{72}{i} = Y$$

where i = interest rate
      Y = years required to double

Rule of 113

$$\frac{113}{i} = Y$$

where i = interest rate
      Y = years required to triple

Semiannual Compounding

$$\frac{R}{2} = i$$

where R = interest rate
      i = semiannual rate

Simple Interest

$$P \times R = I$$

where P = principal
      R = interest rate
      I = interest

Sinking Fund Payments

$$\frac{1}{[(1 + R)^n - 1] \div R} = S$$

where R = periodic interest rate
      n = periods
      S = sinking fund factor

Spread

$$\frac{SP - AP}{AP} = S$$

where SP = sales price
      AP = asked price
      S = spread

Straight-Line Depreciation

$$\frac{B}{P} = D$$

where B = basis of asset
      P = period (in years)
      D = annual depreciation

Tax Benefits From Reporting Losses

$$E \times L = S$$

where E = effective tax rate
      L = net loss from real estate
      S = savings from reduced taxes

Time on the Market

$$SD - LD = T$$

where SD = final sales date
     LD = original listing date
     T = time on the market (number of days)

Total Return

$$\frac{CG + I + T}{Y} = R$$

where CG = capital gains
     I = total net income
     T = net tax benefit (or cost)
     Y = years held
     R = total return

Trial Balance

$$(A - L - N) = P = (R - C - E)$$

where A = asset account balances
     L = liability account balances
     N = net worth account balances
     P = profit (or loss)
     R = revenue account balances
     C = cost account balances
     E = expense account balances

Vacancy Rate

$$\frac{V}{T} = R$$

where V = vacant units
     T = total units
     R = vacancy rate

Volume of a Cylinder

$$\pi \times r^2 \times H = V$$

where π = pi
     r = radius
     H = height
     V = volume

Volume of a Rectangular Solid

$L \times W \times H = V$

where L　=　length
　　　 W　=　width
　　　 H　=　height
　　　 V　=　volume

Weighted Average Interest Rate

$$\frac{(L_1 \times R_1) + (L_2 \times R_2)}{L_t} = A$$

where L_1　=　balance, loan 1
　　　 L_2　=　balance, loan 2
　　　 L_t　=　total balances of loans
　　　 R_1　=　rate on loan 1
　　　 R_2　=　rate on loan 2
　　　 A　=　average interest rate

Weighted Moving Average

$$\frac{V_1 + V_2 + \cdots (V_f \times 2)}{N + 1} = A$$

where V　　　　　 = values in the selected field
　　　 1, 2, ... f = first, second, remaining, and final values
　　　 N　　　　　 = number of values in the field
　　　 A　　　　　 = weighted moving average

Working Capital

$A - L = W$

where A　=　current assets
　　　 L　=　current liabilities
　　　 W　=　working capital

AMORTIZATION TABLES

MONTHLY PAYMENTS

THE TABLE GIVEN HERE provides a *factor* for each dollar borrowed at interest rates from 3.25 percent to 8.00 percent. For example, if your loan amount was $72,500 with 5.25 percent interest over 25 years, you would find the factor for the rate and number of years. Using the row for 5.25 percent and the column for 25 years, you find a factor of 0.00599248. Multiply this by the loan amount to find the required monthly payment:

0.00599248 × $72,500 = $434.45

Using the factor rather than depending on tables of actual payments required is easier and more efficient. Most books of tables show required payments for rounded amounts, so to use such a table, you would need to add together the required payments for $70,000, $2,000 and $500.

Interest	Years to Amortize the Loan					
Rate	5	10	15	20	25	30
3.25	0.01808000	0.00977190	0.00702669	0.00567196	0.00487316	0.00435206
3.50	0.01819174	0.00988859	0.00714883	0.00579960	0.00500624	0.00449045
3.75	0.01830392	0.01000612	0.00727222	0.00592888	0.00514131	0.00463116
4.00	0.01841652	0.01012451	0.00739688	0.00605980	0.00527837	0.00477415
4.25	0.01852956	0.01024375	0.00752278	0.00619234	0.00541738	0.00491940
4.50	0.01864302	0.01036384	0.00764993	0.00632649	0.00555832	0.00506685
4.75	0.01875691	0.01048477	0.00777832	0.00646224	0.00570117	0.00521647
5.00	0.01887123	0.01060655	0.00790794	0.00659956	0.00584590	0.00536822
5.25	0.01898598	0.01072917	0.00803878	0.00673844	0.00599248	0.00552204
5.50	0.01910116	0.01085263	0.00817083	0.00687887	0.00614087	0.00567789
5.75	0.01921677	0.01097692	0.00830410	0.00702084	0.00629106	0.00583573
6.00	0.01933280	0.01110205	0.00843857	0.00716431	0.00644301	0.00599551
6.25	0.01944926	0.01122801	0.00857423	0.00730928	0.00659669	0.00615717
6.50	0.01956615	0.01135480	0.00871107	0.00745573	0.00675207	0.00632068
6.75	0.01968346	0.01148241	0.00884909	0.00760364	0.00690912	0.00648598
7.00	0.01980120	0.01161085	0.00898828	0.00775299	0.00706779	0.00665302
7.25	0.01991936	0.01174010	0.00912863	0.00790376	0.00722807	0.00682176
7.50	0.02003795	0.01187018	0.00927012	0.00805593	0.00738991	0.00699215
7.75	0.02015696	0.01200106	0.00941276	0.00820949	0.00755329	0.00716412
8.00	0.02027639	0.01213276	0.00955652	0.00836440	0.00771816	0.00733765

REMAINING

BALANCE TABLES

WHAT IS LEFT TO PAY

THE TABLES GIVEN HERE show the *percentage* of the loan balance remaining at the end of each year. These tables are based on 30-year amortization for interest rates between 3.25 percent and 8.00 percent.

For example, if you have been making payments on a loan with an original balance of $105,000, and your interest rate is 5.25 percent, the remaining balance at the end of years 10, 15, and 20 would be:

10 years: **81.95%** × **$105,000** = **$86,047.50**
15 years: **68.69%** × **$105,000** = **$72,124.50**
20 years: **51.47%** × **$105,000** = **$54,053.50**

These tables are very instructive, especially for showing how the debt is reduced slowly during the early years and more rapidly in later years. These tables can be used to (1) estimate the effect of accelerating payments, (2) identify equity levels at different years, and (3) compare the differences between interest rates in terms of the speed of paying down the mortgage principal.

Age of Loan	Interest Rate									
	3.25%	3.50%	3.75%	4.00%	4.25%	4.50%	4.75%	5.00%	5.25%	5.50%
1	98.00	98.08	98.16	98.24	98.31	98.39	98.46	98.52	98.59	98.65
2	95.93	96.09	96.25	96.41	96.56	96.70	96.84	96.97	97.10	97.23
3	93.79	94.04	94.27	94.50	94.72	94.93	95.14	95.34	95.54	95.73
4	91.59	91.90	92.21	92.51	92.81	93.09	93.36	93.63	93.89	94.14
5	89.31	89.70	90.08	90.45	90.81	91.16	91.50	91.83	92.15	92.46
6	86.95	87.41	87.86	88.30	88.72	89.14	89.54	89.94	90.32	90.69
7	84.52	85.04	85.58	86.06	86.55	87.03	87.49	87.95	88.39	88.82
8	82.01	82.59	83.17	83.83	84.28	84.82	85.34	85.85	86.35	86.84
9	79.41	80.06	80.69	81.31	81.91	82.51	83.09	83.65	84.21	84.75
10	76.73	77.43	78.11	78.78	79.44	80.08	80.72	81.34	81.95	82.54
11	73.96	74.70	75.44	76.16	76.87	77.56	78.24	78.91	79.57	80.21
12	71.10	71.89	72.66	73.43	74.18	74.92	75.64	76.36	77.06	77.75
13	68.14	68.97	69.78	70.58	71.37	72.15	72.92	73.67	74.41	75.14
14	65.09	65.94	66.79	67.62	68.45	69.26	70.06	70.85	71.63	72.39
15	61.94	62.81	63.68	64.54	65.39	66.23	67.06	67.88	68.69	69.49
16	58.68	59.57	60.46	61.34	62.21	63.07	63.92	64.77	65.60	66.42
17	55.31	56.22	57.11	58.00	58.88	59.76	60.63	61.49	62.34	63.18
18	51.84	52.74	53.64	54.53	55.42	56.30	57.17	58.04	58.90	59.76
19	48.25	49.14	50.03	50.92	51.80	52.68	53.55	54.42	55.28	56.14
20	44.54	45.41	46.28	47.15	48.02	48.89	49.75	50.61	51.47	52.32
21	40.70	41.55	42.40	43.24	44.08	44.93	45.77	46.61	47.45	48.28
22	36.75	37.55	38.36	39.17	39.98	40.79	41.59	42.40	43.21	44.02
23	32.66	33.41	34.17	34.93	35.69	36.45	37.22	37.98	38.75	39.51
24	28.43	29.12	29.82	30.52	31.22	31.92	32.64	33.33	34.04	34.75
25	24.07	24.68	25.30	25.92	26.55	27.18	27.81	28.45	29.08	29.73
26	19.56	20.09	20.61	21.14	21.68	22.22	22.76	23.31	23.86	24.41
27	14.91	15.32	15.75	16.17	16.60	17.03	17.47	17.91	18.36	18.80
28	10.10	10.39	10.69	10.99	11.30	11.61	11.92	12.24	12.55	12.88
29	5.13	5.29	5.45	5.61	5.77	5.93	6.10	6.27	6.44	6.61
30	0	0	0	0	0	0	0	0	0	0

Age of Loan	Interest Rate									
	5.75%	6.00%	6.25%	6.50%	6.75%	7.00%	7.25%	7.50%	7.75%	8.00%
1	98.71	98.77	98.83	98.88	98.93	98.98	99.03	99.08	99.12	99.16
2	97.35	97.47	97.58	97.69	97.79	97.89	97.99	98.08	98.17	98.26
3	95.91	96.08	96.25	96.42	96.57	96.73	96.87	97.01	97.15	97.28
4	94.38	94.61	94.84	95.06	95.27	95.47	95.67	95.86	96.04	96.22
5	92.76	93.05	93.34	93.61	93.88	94.13	94.38	94.62	94.85	95.07
6	91.05	91.40	91.74	92.07	92.38	92.69	92.99	93.28	93.56	93.83
7	89.23	89.64	90.03	90.42	90.79	91.15	91.50	91.83	92.16	92.48
8	87.31	87.77	88.22	88.66	89.08	89.49	89.89	90.28	90.65	91.02
9	85.28	85.79	86.29	86.78	87.25	87.72	88.17	88.60	89.03	89.44
10	83.12	83.69	84.24	84.78	85.30	85.81	86.31	86.79	87.27	87.72
11	80.84	81.45	82.05	82.64	83.21	83.77	84.32	84.85	85.37	85.87
12	78.42	79.08	79.73	80.36	80.98	81.58	82.17	82.75	83.31	83.86
13	75.86	76.56	77.25	77.93	78.59	79.23	79.87	80.49	81.10	81.69
14	73.15	73.89	74.61	75.33	76.03	76.72	77.39	78.06	78.70	79.33
15	70.28	71.05	71.81	72.56	73.30	74.02	74.73	75.43	76.11	76.78
16	67.23	68.04	68.83	69.60	70.37	71.12	71.87	72.60	73.31	74.02
17	64.01	64.84	65.65	66.45	67.24	68.02	68.79	69.55	70.29	71.03
18	60.60	61.44	62.27	63.09	63.89	64.69	65.48	66.26	67.03	67.79
19	56.99	57.83	58.67	59.50	60.32	61.13	61.93	62.72	63.50	64.28
20	53.16	54.00	54.84	55.67	56.49	57.30	58.11	58.91	59.70	60.48
21	49.11	49.94	50.76	51.58	52.39	53.20	54.00	54.79	55.58	56.36
22	44.82	45.62	46.42	47.22	48.01	48.80	49.58	50.36	51.14	51.91
23	40.28	41.04	41.80	42.57	43.32	44.08	44.84	45.59	46.33	47.08
24	35.46	36.18	36.89	37.60	38.31	39.02	39.73	40.44	41.15	41.85
25	30.37	31.01	31.66	32.30	32.95	33.60	34.25	34.89	35.54	36.19
26	24.97	25.53	26.09	26.65	27.22	27.78	28.35	28.92	29.49	30.06
27	19.25	19.71	20.16	20.62	21.08	21.55	22.01	22.48	22.95	23.42
28	13.20	13.53	13.86	14.19	14.52	14.86	15.20	15.54	15.88	16.22
29	6.79	6.97	7.14	7.32	7.51	7.69	7.87	8.06	8.25	8.44
30	0	0	0	0	0	0	0	0	0	0

Glossary

accelerated depreciation   Annual depreciation calculated in such a way that deductions are higher than average in the earlier years and decrease in each subsequent year. Accelerated methods are not allowed for real property but can be used for other classes of property, such as landscaping equipment or vehicles used in real estate investment management.

active participation   The degree of involvement in managing property, for the purpose of qualifying to deduct net losses for tax purposes. This standard requires ongoing involvement in approving tenants, maintaining properties, and approving rent levels and major expenditures.

adjusted gross income (AGI)   Gross income for tax purposes, before deducting tax exemptions and deductions.

adjusted purchase price   The purchase price of property plus closing costs paid by the buyer, inspection fees, prorated expenses, and points paid to lenders.

adjusted sales price   The sale price of property minus the seller's closing costs, which include real estate commissions, inspection fees, repairs, and prorated expenses.

after-tax cash flow   The amount of net positive or negative cash resulting from a property investment, including the benefit or cost from tax calculations.

allocated expenses   Any expenses that cannot be identified as belonging to a specific property, and consequently are spread among two or more investment properties on some basis (such as percentage of gross rent received for each property during the year).

amortization   (1) For a mortgage loan, the reduction over time of the principal due to the lender. The calculated monthly payment is divided between interest (based on the current balance remaining) and principal, which amortizes the loan balance. (2) In tax law, the spreading of an expense over a period of time. Points paid at closing must be amortized each year over the period of repayment of the loan. Prepaid insurance, property taxes, and other expenses are amortized over the months to which the expense applies.

annualization   A return expressed as though an investment had been held for exactly one year. This procedure makes all returns comparable, regardless of how long the property was held.

appraisal   The estimated current market value of property, based on one of several methods. These include the sales or market comparisons, cost, and income methods.

basis   The price of property adjusted upward for closing costs and capital improvements, and adjusted downward for depreciation claimed and for any deferred gain resulting from a 1031 exchange. Basis is used for calculation of capital gains and losses.

cap rate   The capitalization rate, or the return generated by income properties. It compares net operating income to sale prices to estimate value based on a comparison with similar properties in the same area.

capital gain or loss   The profit or loss on investment property. Capital gains on property owned for more than one year are taxed at rates below the ordinary rates applied to other income.

capital improvements   Payments for items that add value to real estate and therefore must be depreciated over a recovery period (as opposed to being deducted as an expense in the year paid).

capitalization   Debt (financing provided by lenders) or equity (investor funds) used to purchase properties. Capitalization may be generated directly from lenders or investors, or indirectly through the use of investment vehicles, such as real estate investment trusts (REITs), mutual funds, and partnerships.

cash flow   The amount of net cash received or paid each month on a real estate investment. When rent receipts are higher than the sum of mortgage payments, operating expenses, and payments for capital improvements, cash flow is positive. When the sum of payments exceeds rental receipts, cash flow is negative.

cash flow projection A calculation of near-future cash receipts and cash payments, used to ensure that an investor can afford a particular investment, given debt service, operating expenses, potential vacancies, and repairs.

construction and development REIT A type of real estate investment trust that specializes in providing financing to builders or developers.

cost method A method used by appraisers to estimate market value, based on the cost to duplicate the same property on land of comparable or identical value.

debt service The payments due on a monthly basis to lenders, consisting of principal and interest and, in many instances, impounds taken by the lender for payments of insurance premiums and property taxes.

declining-balance depreciation A method of calculating annual depreciation in which the depreciation in earlier years is higher than it would be with straight-line rates; under the tax rules, accelerated depreciation can be used for certain classes of assets (but not for real property).

deferred gain A gain on real estate on which the tax liability is put off until sale of a replacement property, under a 1031 exchange.

depreciation (1) In tax law, an annual "recovery" of the investment in real property and other capital assets (but not the value of land). As a noncash expense, depreciation deductions create lower tax liabilities without a corresponding outlay of cash. (2) In appraisal, a calculated annual decline in value resulting from the age, condition, or obsolescence of a property.

discount A price below full market value. In the real estate market, an offer made and accepted that is below the asked price is discounted, and the percentage of difference between the asked price and the sale price is the discount.

economic life In appraisal, the adjusted value of property based on its current condition (not its actual construction age), used as a basis for calculating depreciated market value.

economic rent In appraisal, an assumed market-rate rent used to calculate value using the income method; it can be based on units, rooms, or square feet.

effective age   In appraisal, the age of a property based on its current condition, not its actual year of construction.

effective gross income   The maximum possible rental income from a property, less estimated loss of revenue from vacancies.

effective tax rate   The actual tax rate paid by an individual, based on total taxable income. This rate is used for purposes of assessing the cost or value of investment decisions. It may also be expressed as the rate of tax liability saved or paid on any changes made to the tax due on income as reported.

equity REIT   A real estate investment trust that is designed to assume ownership positions in properties (as opposed to debt positions or leveraged positions); this type of REIT is considered safer than leveraged REIT programs because cash flow requirements exclude debt service.

exchange-traded fund (ETF)   A mutual fund traded on an exchange and specializing in a specific product or range of sectors, such as the real estate industry. The ETF has a fixed portfolio, and shares can be bought or sold on public exchanges.

expense ratio   In appraisal, the relationship between expenses and income, used in the income appraisal method to compare properties to one another.

fair market value   The value of property in today's market based on the average sales of comparable properties in recent months.

gross rent multiplier (GRM)   A factor in appraisal under the income method that is used to establish the values of comparable income properties. Averages of comparable income properties are used to estimate the market value of a subject property.

half-year convention   In depreciation, a method of calculating first-year depreciation. It is based on the assumption that all assets acquired were placed into service exactly one-half of the way through the year, so that first-year depreciation is one-half of what it would have been if the asset had been owned for the full year.

highest and best use   In valuing real estate, a principle stating that property tends to appreciate at the most favorable rate when the land and improvements are used in the best way possible, given zoning, size, location, and attributes.

hybrid REIT   A real estate investment trust that has both equity and debt positions within its portfolio.

illiquidity   The loss, or lack, of liquidity of an investment; a condition in which cash cannot be taken out of the investment without sale or refinancing, or in which no new buyers are available to purchase the investment units a seller wants to sell.

income method   In appraisal, a method used to calculate the market value of properties based on the level of income that is being or that can be generated from a property, given gross rent multipliers for similar properties in the same market.

inventory   Properties available for sale and on the market, calculated in one of two ways: number of properties or months of availability based on typical monthly sales. If 400 homes are currently available and a town's average monthly sales are 100 homes, inventory can be described as 400 properties or as a four-month supply.

investment risk   A risk that investors take when they place capital into any product, including real estate. Attributes define risk; for example, directly owned real estate is illiquid and leverage requires consistent cash flow, but the investment is insured and directly controlled. In comparing one investment to another, it is important that differences in investment risk be taken into account as part of the analysis.

leverage   Investing with borrowed money, such as the mortgaged portion of investment property. The greater the leverage, the greater the cash flow risk; as a result, degrees of leverage may be used to compare the risk levels of various investment strategies.

like-kind exchange (1031 exchange)   A tax provision that allows real estate investors to sell an investment property and replace it with another one. As long as specific rules regarding time and amount are met, the exchange allows the investor to defer the tax liability. The basis in the newly acquired property is reduced by the amount of the deferred gain.

limited partnership   An investment vehicle in which a general partner controls the day-to-day management of properties, and a number of limited partners invest funds. They are "limited" in two respects: They cannot participate in decisions within the partnership, and their maximum risk is limited to their investment capital. Limited partners are not allowed to deduct passive losses, but must apply them against passive gains or carry them forward and apply them against future capital gains upon the sale of properties held within the partnership.

liquidity   (1) In risk analysis, the level of availability of cash in an investment program. In directly owned real estate, liquidity is poor because cash can be removed only through sale or additional borrowing. In stocks, liquidity is high because shares can be bought and sold quickly. Liquidity is a means of comparing investments and judging market risk. (2) In market analysis, a description of whether investments can be sold. Real estate and stocks are highly liquid because new buyers are available. In limited partnerships, there is no ready market, because few new buyers are interested in paying current value for used partnership units; the only way to dispose of them is by selling them at a deep discount. Also called marketability.

margin of profit   In business, the gross or net profit; in real estate, the net difference between the adjusted purchase price and the final adjusted sale price.

marketability   The ease with which an investment can be bought or sold. Stocks are highly marketable because there is an abundance of buyers and sellers, as well as an exchange mechanism. Real estate properties are less marketable because the completion of a sale takes time and involves review steps. Partnership shares have low marketability because there are few full-price buyers for used partnership shares.

market or sales comparison   In appraisal, a method of calculating current market value based on the current market, or by reviewing recent sales of properties of similar size, condition, and location.

market risk   A risk every investor faces, usually related to the possibility of losing money. In real estate, market risk may refer to price changes, trends in rental demand, or cash flow.

material participation   A requirement for investors who directly own property that includes consistent involvement in tenant decisions, approval of expenses, and maintenance. To be considered *materially* involved and qualify for deduction of net losses, the individual must also own no less than 10 percent of the property if it is owned jointly with others.

mid-month convention   In depreciation, a method for figuring the first-year deduction. It assumes that assets acquired during any month were placed into service exactly halfway through that month. There are 24 half-months in every year, so the number of half-months determines the amount of first-year depreciation.

Modified Accelerated Cost Recovery System (MACRS)   The depreciation method currently in use under federal tax rules, in which recovery periods and depreciation methods are specified for different classes of capital assets.

modified adjusted gross income   On an individual's tax return, adjusted gross income without including many of the normal adjustments allowed under the rules. Modified AGI is used to identify income levels in calculating the maximum deduction allowed for real estate losses.

mortgage-backed securities   Debt-based investments in which secured mortgage loans are placed into a package of debts and units are sold to individual investors; a diversified way for individuals to invest in secured debt without having to lend money directly on a single property or to one individual.

mortgage pool   A collection of individual mortgages bundled together, in which individual investors can buy units, like a mutual fund consisting of mortgages rather than stocks or bonds. Mortgage pools are created and managed by federal agencies.

mortgage REIT   A real estate investment trust specializing in lending money to investors, builders, or developers of real estate projects.

negative cash flow   The situation in which monthly expenses and payments are greater than the rental income received from a property.

net breakeven point   The rate of return necessary to break even after the combined effects of inflation and taxes.

net market value   The current market value of a property, after deducting the cost of needed repairs.

occupancy rate   The degree of use of rental property, usually expressed as a percentage of the maximum. For example, a property with four units has a 75 percent occupancy rate when one unit is not occupied. The same situation can also be described by the vacancy rate; the property in this example would have a 25 percent vacancy rate under the conditions described.

passive income or loss   Under federal tax rules, income received or losses incurred by an individual who does not materially participate in the management decisions for the property. Passive losses may not be deducted. They must be applied against passive gains, carried forward to use in future tax years, or used to reduce capital gains when the property is sold.

positive cash flow   The situation in which rental income is greater than the sum of operating expenses, mortgage payments, and other cash outlays.

premium   A price above the asked price. For example, in a seller's market, there may be a number of buyers bidding for a limited number of properties for sale. When a property's price closes above the asked price as a result, the difference is a premium, usually expressed as a percentage of the original asked price.

primary residence   An owner-occupied home; for tax purposes, an individual may have only one *primary* residence. Profits of up to $500,000 may be excluded from taxes when this property is sold. Only one such exclusion is allowed once every two years. For calculating the exclusion, a property must have been used as the primary residence for at least 24 months during the past 60 months.

profitability   In real estate, a measurement of the success of an investment, calculated using one of several methods. Generally, it is the difference between an investment's sale price and its purchase price, adjusted for closing costs, improvements, and depreciation. Profitability may also be based on cash invested (down payment), in which case cash flow is expressed as a percentage of the cash base; or based on annualized capital gains adjusted for interim cash benefits or costs.

prorations   Expenses shared by buyer and seller; they are divided between the two at closing based on the applicable period each is responsible for (usually the number of days); or a partial-month liability for interest on a loan, payable by one side in the transaction to a lender.

ready market   The description of any market in which buyers and sellers can quickly and efficiently locate one another, agree on a price, and complete a transaction.

real estate cycle   The course of supply and demand, reflecting varying degrees of change in attitudes among buyers and sellers and affecting property values.

real estate investment trust (REIT)   An investment vehicle in which investors purchase shares in a trust that is traded on a public stock exchange; the purpose of the REIT is to invest in real estate properties on a specified basis (where properties are identified) or through a blind pool (where a market strategy is spelled out, but the properties themselves are not identified). A

REIT may be classified as equity, mortgage, or hybrid, depending on the investment risk level and the REIT's objective.

recapture   A requirement in tax law that, upon sale of investment property, the sum of depreciation expense is taxed as part of the calculated taxable gain.

recovery period   In depreciation, the number of years over which a capital asset can be depreciated.

replacement value   In appraisal and real estate insurance, the value of property if it were to be replaced in exactly the same condition as today. For example, the quality of workmanship in an older property may be higher than modern standards. Replacement value, as a result, is not the same as current cost or market comparison value.

secondary market   (1) In individual investing, the market for the sale and purchase of existing properties, shares, or units. Stocks have a strong secondary market because shares can be traded easily on the public exchanges, and limited partnerships have a poor secondary market. (2) In the mortgage industry, the collective market for the purchase and bundling of home mortgages. Existing mortgages are sold by lending institutions and formed into mortgage pools. Shares of these pools are then sold to individual investors. This secondary market is operated by several agencies, including the Government National Mortgage Association (GNMA) and the Federal National Mortgage Association (FNMA).

second home   In tax law, a residence used part of the year in conjunction with the primary residence. Individuals are allowed to deduct property taxes and mortgage interest on their primary residence and on one additional property as part of itemized deductions.

secured debt   A debt, such as a mortgage, in which the obligation is secured through equity in some property. In the event of default, the lender has the right to foreclose on the secured property to regain the funds loaned to the property owner or investor.

spread   A calculation used to judge the supply and demand in the current market. It is the difference between average sale prices and average asked prices over a period of time. As the trend in the spread percentage changes, it indicates a corresponding change in market condition.

straight-line depreciation The basic method of calculating annual depreciation expense, in which the depreciable value of the asset is divided by the number of years in the recovery period. The same amount is deducted each year until the asset's basis is fully depreciated.

supply and demand A theory in economics observing that buyers and sellers determine the market value of real estate and other assets. When the number of buyers increases, demand is greater; and when the number of sellers increases, supply is greater. In real estate, supply and demand are found in three specific areas: the market value of properties, the supply of and demand for rental units, and financing, expressed as money supply and affected by changing interest rates.

time on the market The time required for a listed residential property to sell, which is used as an indicator of a market's strength or weakness. In strong seller's markets, the average time properties remain on the market is low, and in strong buyer's markets, the average time on the market increases.

transition Change in a neighborhood or city in which property values move upward or downward. In a positive transition, upgrades and improvements tend to raise average property values, and in a downward transition, neglect causes property values to fall.

turnover An average of the number of times investment capital is replaced over a period of time. The more frequent the turnover, the higher the yield.

useful life In depreciation, an estimated period of years over which an asset may be used in business or investment before it has to be replaced, sold, or abandoned. Useful life determines the recovery period for the asset.

yield Any measurement of profitability or cash flow from an investment; often used as an alternative for *return*. Yield may refer to cash flow as a percentage of cash invested or market value, or to the annualized return upon sale of investment property.

Index

CPSIA information can be obtained at www.ICGtesting.com
Printed in the USA
LVOW04s1526101214

418172LV00018B/1206/P